There's a Puppy in the House
Surviving the First Five Months

Mike Wombacher

Cover Photos: Rose Guilbert
Photos in Book, except where otherwise noted: Rose Guilbert
Cover Design: Rebecca Johnson
Layout: Mike Wombacher
Illustrations: Bruce Henderson

ISBN 0-9713033-1-2

To contact Mike Wombacher:
Website: www.doggonegood.org
415.437.0848

Printed in China by Global PSD

TABLE OF CONTENTS

ACKNOWLEDGMENTS

I have often said that the myth of the self-made man is the product of a divided mind. The truth is that anyone who has ever attained to anything in life has done so because of the help of people and circumstances, both seen and unseen, too numerous to mention. Certainly it has been so in my case.

Foremost amongst such forces in my life has been the influence of Andrew Cohen who has helped to provide context and meaning, vision and inspiration for every aspect of my life.

Next comes my beloved wife Rose who not only took all the photos in this book except where otherwise noted but who has also relentlessly supported my various projects and urged me onward when I thought of giving up.

Then there's Kirk Turner, master dog trainer and great friend. Many years ago he took me under his wing as an apprentice and shared with me every bit of hard won knowledge out of simple and un-adulterated good will. Such kindness and generosity of spirit are sometimes found in the most unlikely of places in a world that often seems to have forsaken the simple virtues in life.

And of course Bruce Henderson whose exquisite illustrations adorn the pages of this book and without whose talent the content that follows would lack a certain lighthearted playfulness.

Lastly, a debt of gratitude is owed to those generous clients who offered photographs and volunteered their pups for training photos, especially Carl and Burr Diehl and their wonderful dog Truffle, and Tanya Miller with her pup Wrigley.

And finally a special thanks to Chris and Candy Berg without whose generous support this book might never have come to be published in the first place.

About The Author

Michael Wombacher is a San Francisco resident who has been involved with dogs for over twenty years in a variety of capacities and at this writing he has performed well over ten-thousand in home behavioral consultations covering the entire spectrum of dog behavior from the mundane to the bizarre. He is an author and lecturer and has also taught classes, trained other trainers, helped run kennels as well as his own small-scale boarding and training operation. His first book *There's a Baby in the House: Preparing your Dog for the Arrival of your Child* has received nationwide praise in major magazines including Dog World and Fit Pregnancy.

Mike has been certified as an expert in dog behavior by the California Superior Court and does occasional work evaluating dogs in legal matters. He has also been featured on Fox 5 Television's Good Day New York, San Francisco's Channel 7 News as well as radio stations nationwide and has trained dogs for high profile celebrities in the entertainment and financial worlds such as Robin Williams, Sharon Stone, Barry Levinson, Charles Schwab and Michael Tilson Thomas.

His training approach focuses on channeling a dog's natural drives and instincts into behaviors acceptable in the human pack primarily through the principles of positive reinforcement and operant conditioning as well as through methods that appeal to the dog's canine sensibilities.

His training methods are so effective and his style so clear that Michael Tilson Thomas, music director of the San Francisco Symphony and one of the great classical musicians of our time, commented that "Michael Wombacher is a maestro of dog trainers. His clarity of thinking, sense of humor and skills in communicating make dog training fun for both pet and pet lover."

FOREWORD

So you've gotten a puppy. He's cute and sweet and not listening at all. That little angel of yours now seems like a devil. Suddenly all the "Awwws" are being replaced with "Oh Nos!" Not another chewed shoe, soiled rug or night of endless crying in the crate. Now what do you do? An owner's manual for puppyhood sure would be handy.

Thankfully you've got one right in your hands. Mike Wombacher's "There's a Puppy in the House" shows you what to do when the honeymoon is over. His is a practical guidebook for the real life situations and experiences you will encounter with your cuddly canine. It will quickly become apparent that training a puppy is as much about training him as it is about training yourself. And figuring out how he will fit into your life – not how your life will revolve around his – is no small part of this.

Over the course of many years, I have witnessed the benefit of early and consistent training, socialization and behavior modification through observing the development of the hundreds of puppies that have passed through my puppy preschool program. And of course, the importance of owner-reinforcement of the new behaviors cannot be overemphasized. "There's a Puppy in the House" is a roadmap for this type of training and in Mike you will find a very apt and qualified guide.

It's very easy, despite our best intentions, to do the wrong things with our pups. They're adorable and we want to give them the world, letting them do whatever they want and often letting them get away with murder. This book walks you through the urge to spoil your furry friend to his detriment and will enable you to create the ideal relationship with your pup, without diminishing the joy of puppyhood at all. Mike shows us that when common sense, consistency, and boundaries are applied up-front they lay the foundation for an enjoyable, life-long relationship with our pets. "There's a Puppy in the House" will supply you with practical, real world solutions to training your pup and plenty of ideas for integrating him or her into your lives. It is an invaluable tool for the journey though puppyhood.

Laura Hawkins-Smith
Owner, K9 to 5 Dog Day Care
Co-founder BAD RAP and Bay Area Bullydog Alliance Rescue Groups

INTRODUCTION

Congratulations! If you're reading this you're probably the proud owner of a new puppy and if you're like most new puppy owners you'll find yourself tossed back and forth between joy and exasperation. On the one hand those little bundles of fur are so unbearably cute that you can barely stand it and on the other they're eliminating all over your house, barking for attention, nipping and biting at you or your kids and chewing everything in sight. What's a caring owner to do?

The purpose of this book is to help new puppy owners through the first five months of their pup's life. While your dog will hopefully be with you for twelve years, fifteen years, or perhaps even longer, what you do during the first four months will profoundly impact both his relationship with you and his orientation to life as a whole. You see, between the time your pup is seven weeks old and the time he becomes approximately four to four and a half months of age he is in what is referred to as his *critical socializing period*. What this means is that anything your pup learns and adapts to during this period will be pretty much hard wired for life and anything that he does not learn during this period he will have an increasingly difficult time adapting to as he gets older. That is not to say that, "you can't teach an old dog new tricks." You most certainly can. However, it is *infinitely* easier to simply start your pup off on the right paw by channeling his natural drives and instincts into behaviors acceptable in his new human pack, your family.

Well, hello there!

In what follows I will discuss issues of temperament, functional issues such as housebreaking, chewing, and barking, relationship issues that revolve around trust and respect, primarily puppy biting and rebelliousness, and environmental issues that determine your pup's relationship to a broad range of experiences he will encounter in life such as grooming, boarding, city noises, other dogs, people and more. I will also introduce and describe fundamental obedience training exercises that will prepare your pup for more formal obedience as he gets older.

In the last section I have outlined a timeline that will help you to understand when in your pup's development you should introduce the various elements discussed in this book. And finally, throughout this book I've tried, in my own cornball way, to inject some humor into its writing, bearing in mind the comment of a former mentor that "if you don't have a sense of humor it just isn't funny."

Before getting started I'd like to make a couple of comments on writing style. First, there are there are occasions throughout this book where I repeat myself. The reason for this is twofold. That is, some things bear repeating simply for emphasis but I also understand that certain readers may just skip around this book looking for answers to particular problems and I want to be sure that the points that are repeated are likely to be read by all. Second, there is the issue of gender. Throughout what follows I refer to both dogs and owners as "he." I assure you, this is not due to any gender bias on my part but simply due to limitations in the English language. Since we have no gender neutral personal pronouns available to us I have chosen to uniformly refer to everyone as "he" for the simple reason that I am a "he" and it's the most comfortable for me. I hope the reader understands and takes no offense.

Before diving into the nuts and bolts of my program there are a number of issues and principles that every new puppy owner should be familiar with. Since an understanding of these will build a solid foundation on which to develop your relationship with your new pup why don't we start there?

THE TIMELINE!

One of the best features of this book is the puppy primer timeline located on page 211. Here you will find a step by step, day by day, week by week schedule of how and when to implement everything in this book. That means that you need not read this book cover to cover and then try to figure out what to do when, you can simply start with the timeline and work from there. In this way you'll read exactly what you need when you need.

The only sections I recommend everyone read from the get go is the **Before Getting Started** Section that follows immediately after this Introduction.

BEFORE GETTING STARTED – A FEW THINGS YOU SHOULD KNOW

TEMPER TO THE TEMPERAMENT

Every puppy has a *fundamental genetic predisposition* with respect to his temperament, temperament being loosely defined as his basic orientation and attitude to the experience of being alive. From an evolutionary and behavioral standpoint this makes perfect sense. That is, in order to have a smoothly functioning pack of dogs the temperaments of the members should range across the spectrum of possibilities otherwise peaceful or even successful coexistence might be pretty difficult. For example, if you had twelve dogs, all extremely confident and dominant, you'd have nothing but fights all day. Since they'd always be at odds, endlessly quibbling about status, nothing would ever get done. (Sounds a lot like what goes on in Washington, doesn't it?). They'd never be able to organize a successful hunt and soon they'd all starve, each still a legend in their own mind. On the other hand, if the entire pack were comprised of rather meek, subordinate types they'd never muster the collective courage to leave the den. The net result – they'd starve in the safety of that den. In other words, you need a mix of temperamental predispositions to make a pack run like a well-oiled machine. And truthfully, is it any different with humans?

Ranger is twelve weeks old and ready for training!

Photo: Mike Wombacher

At any rate, in order to smoothly introduce your pup into the human world you must take this predisposition into account. Every puppy is an individual and while the principles set forth in this book apply equally to all the way they're implemented will vary somewhat. In other words, you must temper your training approach to the temperament of your pup.

That having been said, please bear in mind that the genetically based component of your pup's personality is simply a "predisposition," not a hardwired fact – yet. Every puppy, no matter what temperamental extreme he may be coming from, can be brought toward the middle of the temperamental spectrum through intelligent handling, guidance and training. It's the old "nature vs. nurture" situation. In this case "nature" is molded by "nurture" to develop a well-balanced pup that can be readily integrated into your life.

For example, if you have a puppy that seems to be afraid of everything you can, through intense socialization and systematic desensitization (which will be discussed in detail later), create a much more outgoing, or at least less tentative, disposition in him. Thus, while his basic orientation toward novel experiences will always be a bit on the cautionary side, this will neither stop him from enjoying the experience of living nor from being a wonderful companion for you.

All that having been said, let's take a look at the most common temperamental predispositions found in young puppies.

The Shy Pup

The shy pup is, well…shy. When he encounters novel situations he's, at the very least, tentative. He may even choose to avoid the situation altogether rather than risk anything by exploring it. Often the first place he'll seek to hide out from the sometimes emotionally challenging experiences of life is in your lap or behind your legs.

A puppy like this needs lots of encouragement and patience to convince him that life is not such a scary affair. *However, what he does not need is an overly protective parent.* If, every time your pup is scared and comes running to you, you pick him up to protect him he'll simply never muster the nerve to go and investigate new situations. After all, you're positively reinforcing, albeit unintentionally, his fearful behavior. Instead what he'll adopt is a behavioral disposition known as *learned helplessness.* That is, he'll become convinced that he's always helpless and that he should forever shrink from novel situations. As this pup becomes a dog he will be highly likely to develop an attitude known as *fear aggression*, arguably the most common type of aggression one encounters with a dog and also one of the most difficult to resolve.

Moreover, often a fearful pup never gets the opportunity to vigorously interact with other puppies during his critical socializing period. The upshot of this can be that he'll not learn what is known as *bite inhibition* from the other pups. In other words, play with other pups gives him feedback as to when he's bitten too hard. The other pup will either return the favor or run for his life. Either way your pup has lost a playmate. This teaches him to be more careful. Since your pup is never going to be allowed to bite you, as you'll see shortly, it's important that he learn bite inhibition from other pups. Once a pup is past his critical socializing period it's pretty well impossible for him to learn bite inhibition. The net result is that often a fearful pup that grows up without having learned bite inhibition will, when cornered, lash out with a serious attack.

So what can you do to avoid this? There are basically two types of responses available to you: ignore him or change the mood. Let's take a look at each in turn. If you find that your pup is suddenly alarmed by something and he comes running over to you to hide between your legs, simply ignore him. That's right. Do nothing. Does that seem kind of cold? Perhaps, but it really isn't. Keep in mind, you don't want to positively reinforce his fear. *Never, under any circumstances coddle, comfort, or in any way reassure a fearful pup.* If you do you're guaranteed to propel this behavior through the roof. If your pup wants to hide between your legs, by all means let him, but go no further than that (unless there really is something dangerous, of course). Allow him to view you as a home base, a safe place from which he can venture out and explore the world, but certainly not as a place to run to and hide away from the experience of life.

NEVER CODDLE A FEARFUL PUP

If you have a shy or fearful puppy try not to coddle or comfort him everytime he's scared. Instead, change the mood by being suddenly positive and upbeat. Do not buy into his fear. Rather lift him out of his gloom with a positive attitude, a handclap and a cheerful voice.

Imbue him with some of your positivity rather than climbing into his emotional black hole with him and in due course he'll gain the confidence to venture forth on his own.

TOO CUTE FOR WORDS!

Puppies are too cute for words. It is often only their unbearable cuteness that gives us the patience to deal with their antics during their first few months with us.

The other available option is to *change the mood.* In other words, rather than buying into his anxiety-ridden state, create an entirely new atmosphere. Suddenly, instead of speaking to him in cooing and soothing sounds, become upbeat and happy. Clap your hands, speak to him in a high-spirited tone of voice and move his attention into a game or some other fun interaction with you. Use a little of your positive energy to lift him out of his funk. Have you ever had a rotten day where everything in you wants to just draw the curtains, stay home and hide out? And have you ever had a friend come over and drag you out to the movies only to find that with a change of set and setting the gloom begins to lift like the fog under a midday sun? Be that friend to your pup! Working with him like this will, in due course, brighten his attitude and confidence level in relation to life as a whole.

With the shy pup you'll want to spend lots of time and energy pursuing the socialization and desensitization exercises outlined in the pages that follow.

The Pushy Pup

The pushy pup demands. Demands what? Well, pretty much everything. He's constantly bringing you toys to play with, nipping at your shoes and pants, barking when he wants attention, in short, constantly seeking out new strategies to be the center of the known universe. Because he's so cute and fluffy it's hard not to comply with his every wish. After all, what harm could that do? Actually, plenty. While it's certainly okay to play with your pup in all sorts of ways it's not a good idea to teach him that he can make demands on you. Keep in mind, your pup will only be a pup a very short time. Before you know it he'll be a full-grown adolescent (read punk) dog who will have solidly internalized the attitude "I demand I get." Do I really need to spell out the kind of problems a now large teenage dog with this sort of outlook can create for you? I don't think it'll take a huge stretch of the imagination to fill in this picture.

With the pushy puppy you'll need to be a little assertive, being sure that he learns to go through you in order to get anything he values. The moment he learns obedience commands, even on the most rudimentary level, be sure to demand them from him in exchange for anything nice that he gets from you.

I want to play...now!

While this is good policy with any pup, it's especially important with the pushy pup. A pushy pup that grows up out of control stands a high likelihood of becoming what's known as dominant aggressive as he matures. Spare yourself this headache and begin curbing his pushy habits early on. In subsequent sections of this book I will discuss both handling and obedience exercises and with the pushy pup you should be especially diligent in applying these early and often.

I WANT, I WANT, I WANT!

With the pushy puppy you'll need to be a little assertive, being sure that he learns to go through you in order to get anything he values. The moment he learns obedience commands, even on the most rudimentary level, be sure to demand them from him in exchange for anything nice that he gets from you.

The Velcro Pup

The Velcro pup is a variation on a theme, i.e., the shy pup. You can't seem to shake the Velcro pup. He's always underfoot, glued to you as if he were worried that if he takes his little brown eyes off you for even a moment you'll disappear into the void forever.

This pup needs to learn that fun stuff also happens away from you. Puppy play groups, interactive dog toys and any enjoyable activity at some distance from you will help him enormously. You'll also need to be extra diligent with him when it comes to teaching him to tolerate time alone. In the chapters that follow you'll find ample information on how to deal with each of these situations.

With this pup you must resist the temptation to indulge him in lots of excessive affection as this will only make him more dependent and the admonition never to comfort, coddle or reassure him if he's ever fearful applies doubly.

PLEEZE DON'T LEAVE ME!

This pup needs to learn that fun stuff also happens away from you. Puppy play groups, interactive dog toys and any enjoyable activity at some distance from you will help him enormously. You'll also need to be extra diligent with him when it comes to teaching him to tolerate time alone. Failing to do so now could create problems with separation anxiety later, and this is one of the most difficult behavior problems to resolve.

The Piranha Pup

The piranha pup is another variation on a theme, i.e., the pushy pup. This pup is prone to extreme fits of temper when he doesn't get his way. He'll often shows such signs of viciousness that the owners are left in a state of shock, wondering if they acquired some kind of psychotic demon dog out of a Stephen King novel. With his curled lips, vicious snarl and uninhibited willingness to bite, you might even swear that you could see a red glow in his otherwise soulful eyes. Surprisingly, almost all of these pups can be quickly brought past their fits of temper and will grow up to be perfectly nice adult dogs in due course. However, this requires special diligence in practicing the handling exercises that are discussed in a later section of this book, exercises that are specifically designed to make the pup tolerant and learn that biting humans is never okay under any circumstances, period.

The Aloof Pup

The aloof pup just can't be bothered…with anything. Now, having such a pup doesn't necessarily create any behavioral problems but it does occasionally create frustrated owners. "I wish he'd play more," "he just doesn't look like he's having any fun," "does he love me?" are what's commonly heard.

The aloof pup more or less lives in his own little world. I once had a German Shepherd like this. He wasn't all that interested in any of the common dog games like fetch, chase or kill the squirrel. What was worse was that he

wasn't particularly interested in being petted by me. It almost seemed as if he'd tolerate it in order to do me a favor. However, after five minutes he felt compelled to go find his own place to lie down and perform what he must have thought was his mission in life: guard duty.

With a pup like this you'll have to work to find activities that you can do together. If your pup is from a working breed that's got an inclination to perform a particular type of function try to channel those drives into games together. In a later section I'll offer a brief discussion of dog activities such as tracking, agility and others that can help in this area.

The Busybody Pup

The busybody pup is like the Energizer Bunny. He just keeps going and going and going. Some people might call him hyper but I'll just call him …inquisitive… yeah, that's it. This puppy needs lots of stimulation but he also needs to accept certain limits. It's very easy to over stimulate a pup like this by sending him to doggie day care every day, taking him to the beach for two hours five times a week and generally going to great lengths just trying to wear him out. In short, it's very easy to habituate him to that level of stimulation which can cause enormous problems when that level of stimulation is absent.

With this pup you'll need to balance his need for exercise and sensory input with down time. Creatively combining outings, games, and social activities with focused obedience and down time, all of which will be discussed shortly, should help to keep this pup manageable. If all else fails, elephant tranquilizers should do the trick (just kidding, of course.)

The Ordinary Pup

There are some pups that don't seem to display any of the characteristics discussed above. They are neither shy nor pushy, just appropriately curious. They neither cling to you nor ignore you, but seem to have just the right mix of interest in you and interest in their environment. While they are active, they are not frenetically so and while they stand their ground in many situations they never act aggressively towards humans or animals. If you have one of these pups consider yourself lucky because rather than being ordinary he is actually somewhat out of the ordinary. A pup like this will adapt readily to everything outlined in this book and, when properly raised, will be unlikely to ever create real problems for you.

A Note on Small Pups

Small dogs get away with murder. Why? Because they're small. How often have you heard someone say that they hate small dogs because they're so yippy or so nasty? I hear it all the time. Well, there's nothing inherent in a small dog that makes him unpleasant other than his ability to get away with murder. People tolerate behaviors from little dogs for which they would have euthanized their Rottweiler long ago. Never forget that every dog is essentially cut from the same cloth as his wolf forbearers including your little Chihuahua.

In other words, if you want a well-adjusted small dog please hold him to the same standard as you would any other dog. Now, I'm not suggesting that your little Chihuahua should catch a Frisbee like your Labrador (this would obviously kill him), but behaviorally please do not make any exceptions for him based on size. A little Napoleon you can definitely live without.

What's Your Temperament?

A great deal of what makes a relationship between a dog and his owner work is how well the temperament of the two are matched. In fact, this is the single largest determinant of whether the relationship will work or end in discord.

That having been said, there's also the element of "you do what you can and you get what you get." In other words, there are lots of things you can do to stack the deck in favor of getting the puppy you want but in the end you have to leave room for the unknowns. Is it any different when you have kids?

I suspect that if you're reading this book you've already gotten a pup and the reason I'm bringing this up is to get you to pause for a moment and investigate your own emotional investment in your pup's disposition. Perhaps you wanted a really big, tough Doberman but ended up with one rather on the shy side. Or perhaps it's the other way around. Perhaps you wanted a very demure, reclining little lapdog but instead your Lhasa Apso is aloof and only interested in driving off all intruders whose presence is apparent to his acute sensory apparatus. Rather than being frustrated by this turn of events I would encourage you to be a little psychologically and emotionally flexible. As I mentioned above, there are a great many things you can do to shape a dog's disposition in the direction you want, and a good number of them are outlined in this book. However, you should also be prepared to make a few adjustments in order to attune yourself to your pup. Trying to force him into a suit that doesn't fit will neither make him comfortable nor you happy. Meeting in the middle will.

Conversely, don't take a negative behavioral leaning on the part of your pup and encourage it because it suits some pre-conceived idea you might have of what you want. For instance, if you've got a shy puppy and kind of like that emotional dependency, please resist the temptation to nurture that habit. Or, in the same vein, if you've got a suspicious puppy who's inclined towards an occasional show of aggression and you really wanted a tough protective dog, please resist the temptation to reinforce those traits in him. Trust me, catering to these tendencies will lead to disaster. Please be honest with yourself and try, using the suggestions outlined in this book, to move your puppy towards the middle of the temperament spectrum, an area where all can live happily ever after.

Dogs, Temperaments & Where To Read About Them.

For excellent information regarding the temperamental predispositions of dogs, the personalities of their owners and the interactions between them see Myrna Milani's books, The Body Language and Emotions of Dogs and Dogsmart. They are well written, incisive, and entertaining.

When considering temperamental predispositions it's also a good idea to have some idea as to the varying temperamental tendencies you'll find in different breeds and consider how these will fit with your personality. An excellent resource is Daniel Tortora's The Right Dog for You as is Your Purebred Puppy: A Buyer's Guide, by Michele Welton.

When choosing a puppy and attempting to assess its temperamental predisposition there are a number of puppy personality tests that can help you look into the future. For more information on puppy temperament tests please see Puppy Personality Profile by Wendy Volhard. Since this little book is hard to find you might also check the internet for information regarding puppy temperament testing.

An excellent place to find all these books and many others dealing with every conceivable dog issue is Direct Book Services. They can be reached at 800-776-2665 Monday through Friday, 7:30 a.m. to 4:00 p.m. Pacific Time or at www.dogwise.com.

A Few More Things to Know

 As you've seen on the previous pages, puppies can and do vary greatly in their temperamental predispositions. In what follows I'll be sure, where appropriate, to discuss the importance such differences have in relation to the various training and handling exercises covered in this book. Also, be aware that the temperamental predispositions delineated above can, to some degree, coexist in the same puppy. For example, you can have a shy puppy that's also a busybody or a pushy pup that's sometimes shy. As you get to know your pup you'll see for yourself what he's made of and be able to adjust your training approach accordingly.

In addition to the differences in puppies that I've discussed so far, they also have a great deal in common. Let's take a look at some of the commonalities your pup shares with every other pup that ever was or will be. For starters…

Your Pup Needs to Sleep…A lot

Little puppies are cute…really cute. In fact they're so cute that it seems someone always wants to play with them. This is especially true of homes with children. No sooner does one person put a puppy down than another wants to pick him up and cuddle or play with him. Of course, to some degree this is fine. Your new pup needs to get to know everyone and learn to feel comfortable with them.

However, your puppy needs sleep, and lots of it. Please make sure he gets it. Most of the nutrients he absorbs during the early stages of his life go into supporting his needs for growth and what's left over goes into puppy activity. Sleeping allows for the absorption of vital nutrients that foster your pup's physical development. Dis-

---

TIRED DOGS ARE GOOD DOGS

Sleep and exercise are both integral parts of a pup's healthy development. However, too much exercise is not a good thing. Your pup is not a superathlete. Please don't take him on three mile runs or to the beach for four hours. In time he'll be able to join you in these things but overdoing it too soon can damage his development and spoil his fun. For now two to four exercise periods of five to twenty minutes apiece should more than suffice. Also, look to play on soft surfaces and avoid concrete, hardwood floors, etc.

turbing that sleep inhibits this process. It is not uncommon for young pups to sleep as much as eighteen hours a day (nighttime included) and the old adage to let sleeping dogs lie certainly applies here. In short, please resist the temptation to wake the pup every time you're overcome by his cuteness and have an irresistible urge to pet him or play with him. That having been said, it is also true that...

Your Pup Needs To Play

It is through play that your puppy will learn a great deal about his relationship with you and the other family members as well as pets in your household. Play is an extremely important part of his life and should definitely not be ignored. Since a good deal of your initial interactions with your pup will revolve around establishing behavior guidelines and limits it is important to keep this in mind when you play with him. In this book you'll find numerous examples of how to interact with your pup in both playful and constructive ways that support all your behavioral goals without foregoing the fun of having a puppy.

In addition to play...

Go get it, boy!

Your Pup Needs To Explore

In the same way that your pup learns about his relationship with you through play he begins to develop a relationship to his environment through exploration. While all your pup's explorations should be carefully supervised, as you'll see shortly, they should also be frequent and diverse.

Extensive laboratory research has definitively proven that animals that are raised in what is called an "enriched environment" literally alter the physical development of their brain in a very positive way. The number of neurons and the synaptic connections between them have been shown to increase directly in proportion to the diversity and frequency of environmental input. This is one of those instances where more definitely is better. In this connection, I'll have a lot to say in the pages that follow regarding your pup's needs for socialization and exposure to his environment. Of course, a related item to consider is that in order for him to learn what's appropriate behavior in his environment...

Your Pup Needs Structure, Guidance, and Authority

In many ways puppies are like young children. When they come into your life they know absolutely nothing about the world in which they live. In order to gather information about this world they begin to explore and unconsciously look for behavior boundaries. Like children, if they fail to come into contact with such boundaries they start pushing harder, and then harder, until they're literally spinning out of control. Thus your job as parent is to let your pup know, through structure, guidance and authority, where those boundaries lie. It would be no different in a dog pack. In that context, young pups very quickly learn the contours of those boundaries, first from mom and then from their littermates and other pack members. This, of course, is an evolutionary and survival imperative. Without such boundaries few young pups would grow up to be adult dogs. That having been said, let's take quick look at each of the three elements.

First, your pup needs structure and routine in his life. Dogs are creatures of habit. Whatever they do three or four times in a predictable sequence they'll be likely to expect again. Such structure , routine and predictability represent safety for your pup. Did you ever see that movie "Groundhog Day" with Bill Murray? It's the film where Bill Murray lives the same day over and over again. Each day is identical to the day before. This is a dog's dream life. Nothing would make him happier than to have every day be predictably the same. In the pages that follow, I'll speak a great deal about how to regulate your pup's life in such a way as to make it sensible and easy to interpret for him.

LEADERSHIP

In many ways puppies are like young children. When they come into your life they know absolutely nothing about the world in which they live. In order to gather information about this world they begin to explore and unconsciously look for behavior boundaries. Like children, if they fail to come into contact with such boundaries they start pushing harder, and then harder, until they're literally spinning out of control. Thus your job as parent is to let your pup know, through structure, guidance and authority, where those boundaries lie.

Second, your pup needs guidance from you. You should get him used to taking direction from you early on by being there at critical junctures to guide him in the right direction and help him to make appropriate decisions. In this respect I'll soon be talking about the need for intense supervision in the early stages of your pup's life and a little bit further on about using rudimentary obedience exercises as forms of guidance.

Third, your pup needs authority. This is a point that bears dwelling on because of its extreme importance. Dogs are, by nature, "pack animals." In order to

Wolves are the common ancestor of all dogs from the tiniest little toys to the largest of the giant breeds.

THE PACK MENTALITY OF DOGS

A great deal has been written and said these days about the need to play the role of alpha dog for your pup or, to put it differently, to be his boss. Let's take a quick look at why dogs operate this way.

From Chihuahuas to Great Danes, all dogs are genetically speaking approximately eighty five percent wolf. This means that a great deal of their behaviors derive directly from their wolf forbearers. Wolves organize themselves into packs to hunt large game and since no single wolf can take down an elk teamwork is essential. Thus a survival imperative for wolves is to hunt cooperatively as a group and without structure and organization such an undertaking is impossible. In order for such a group to function smoothly hierarchy is required. Moreover, such hierarchy cannot be established through physical force since this might result in injured pack members. Of course, if pack members are injured because of infighting they can't hunt and this could mean the demise of the entire pack. Thus wolves, and their canine cousins, have worked out elaborate routines of dominance, submission, and ritualized aggression (violent encounters that are literally more bark than bite, leaving few if any injuries) which they use to assert and communicate social position without actually having to hurt each other. Since dogs transfer their pack instincts to their human group a great part of intelligent dog ownership involves taking advantage of these innate understandings in order to effectively communicate with our dogs. Throughout this book you'll learn how to do exactly that.

minimize conflict and function smoothly, packs are structured hierarchically. In other words, not only do they have a leader but all pack members relate to each other as either "higher ranking," or "lower ranking." To put it differently, members are either "dominant" or "submissive" in relation to one another. A dog that does not perceive leadership in his environment will assume that the role, by default, is his. The concept of egalitarianism not only does not exist for him but can be frightening. As I've said elsewhere, "while in the human world equality might equal justice, in the canine world, equality equals violence." In other words issues of equality may ultimately have to be settled via physical force. While this applies more to adolescent and adult dogs – which your pup will be sooner than you think – I hope you'll take the point. A huge part of puppy ownership revolves around providing effective leadership and playing the role of the so-called "alpha dog." As you will see in the pages that follow, authority does not equate with being the bully and "showing him who's boss" in the way that that statement is usually understood. It equates with effective and well-balanced leadership based on understanding and compassion. In the end it's your authority that ties together structure and guidance and makes them meaningful for your pup.

In order for you to effectively implement structure, guidance and authority...

Your Pup Needs You To Communicate

"What we have here is a failure to communicate" were the warden's famous words to Paul Newman in *Cool Hand Luke* before he gave him "ten days in the box." Since a great deal of dog-owner problems stem from the failure to communicate let's take a quick look at our means of communication and how to best use them.

INTERESTING RESOURCES

If you'd like to learn more about canine body language and communication you might find the following books interesting:

Turid Rugaas, Calming Signals.

> Filled with interesting and useful information though somewhat poorly written and produced, this inexpensive little book should be read by anyone interested in learning more about canine body language.

Myrna Milani, The Body Language and Emotions of Dogs.

> Excellent and in-depth overview of dog-owner communication issues. Definitely not a quick reference. Wonderful case histories from the author's practice make this book fun to read and understandable.

Roger Abrantes, Dog Language: An Encyclopedia of Canine Behavior,

> In depth, though quite academic, overview of canine body language. Definitely for the serious student.

Stanley Coren, How to Speak Dog: Mastering the Art of Dog-Human Communication.

Another, perhaps more fringe, but extremely interesting book is **Rupert Sheldrake's** Dogs That Know When Their Owners Are Coming Home: And Other Unexplained Powers of Animals. Sheldrake, though shunned by conventional academic scientists, has done extremely interesting research on communication outside the means of the sensory apparatus and has theorized the existence of "morphogenetic fields" to account for information transfer that cannot be explained with conventional methods.

Most of these titles should be available from Direct Book Services at 800-776-2665, Monday through Friday, 7:30 a.m. - 4:00 p.m., PT, or at www.dogwise.com.

TONES OF VOICE

Generally speaking, a puppy will distinguish meaning between three tones of voice:

1) Low pitch equals reprimand or displeasure.

2) Medium or ordinary is just that and generally interpreted as a means to convey basic information.

3) High pitched is interpreted as an invitation to play.

I don't know if dogs are psychic as some "animal communication experts" here in California seem to think, but I do know that they're perceptive to a degree that is almost unimaginable to human beings. When it comes to observing us they miss very little. On the contrary, when it comes to observing them we miss almost everything. In a way this is understandable. Dogs have relatively simple lives and we tend to be the center of their world. We, on the other hand, have extraordinarily complex lives of which the pup is merely one small component. Moreover, dogs communicate primarily through observing each other's body language, while people communicate primarily through spoken words, relegating other observations to the very back of their minds. Since your pup notices the slightest changes in your posture, attitude, eye movements and a great deal more you should use these elements to your advantage. Let's take a quick look at some major means of communication and how to effectively use them.

What are your means of communication? Your voice, your arms and hands, your eyes, your leash and your overall demeanor all send signals to your pup about your mood and intent. Use them to your advantage. Let's take a look at each in turn.

As far as your voice is concerned, your pup, by the time he arrives at your home, has learned from mom and littermates to identify three different tones and attach meaning to them. He'll tend to identify a low tone of voice as a reprimand or a general sign of your displeasure. A medium or ordinary tone he'll view as one intended to convey some functional information and a high-pitched tone will be interpreted as an invitation to play. A common issue that comes up in this regard is that many women, when they get upset, tend to raise the pitch in their voice, as do children. Since the pup might interpret this as an invitation to play it should come as no surprise when he doesn't take the reprimand seriously.

Simply changing the tone of voice usually corrects the problem. There are endless similar examples.

Your arms, hands overall posture and attitude of your body also communicate a great deal of information to your pup. For example, approaching him from the front and/or above will be interpreted as very dominant while approaching him from the side and underneath will be interpreted as less dominant. A calm, matter of fact, almost stoic approach to your pup will tend to produce a similar state in him while a great deal of fast and wild movement will excite him into play. In subsequent chapters you'll learn both handling exercises and hand signals that will take advantage of your pup's alertness to handling and body postures and help you to put yourself in a leadership position in his mind.

Another extremely important means of communication are your eyes. Any pup, as well as adult dog, will always be extremely conscious of what you're telling him with your eyes. Generally speaking, direct eye contact will be viewed as very dominant and potentially confrontational while an aversion of eye contact will send the opposite message. This area can get a little tricky in your efforts at inter-species communication since for humans direct eye contact can be not only confrontational but intimate as well. In the section on obedience training I'll teach you to teach your pup to understand that eye contact from you is not always confrontational and to judge its meaning based on the overall context of a situation.

HERE'S LOOKIN' AT YOU

Since most pups view eye contact as challenging, it's important to teach them to both accept eye contact from us as a sign of affection and to know when it is meant as a reprimand.

While it's certainly never okay to give a young puppy a harsh leash correction, the leash is another way of transmitting information to your pup. Slight nudges, gentle prods and occasionally a steady pull are all appropriate ways of sending messages to your pup. In the sections below you'll learn a number of ways of using your leash to communicate with your pup in acceptable and humane ways.

The tools outlined above – your voice, body, eyes, overall attitude and leash – should be used creatively, positively and in concert to send an overall and consistent message to your pup. Effectively pulling these elements together not only allows you to provide structure, guidance and authority for him, it will forge an incredibly strong bond between the two of you as well. In addition to the functional elements of raising a puppy, the forging of this bond is one of the primary purposes of everything that's contained in this book.

One final thing in relation to communication. Your pup lives very much in the *now!* He does not consider what he did two seconds ago and isn't remotely concerned with what's going to happen a millisecond from now. His attention is fully riveted to the present moment. What that means is that you'll have to keep your communications with him in line with what's happening *now*. In other words, you'll have to able to shift and move in accordance with your pup's changing emotional and behavioral states seamlessly. If your communication with him is based on something he was doing a few seconds back it might be completely useless in relation to what he's up to right now. While this principle holds true across the board it is especially important with regard to reprimands which will be discussed shortly.

Needless to say, communication is fundamental to any learning and your pup has lots of learning to do. Therefore, let's take a quick look at how learning works for him:

Your Pup Learns By Association

When two events happen simultaneously or in close proximity to one another your pup begins to build a connection between them in his mind. If this happens on a consistent basis he will begin to anticipate the pattern. Of course this principle cuts both ways in the course of raising your puppy. For example, if every time you come home you scream at the pup and hit him with a rolled up newspaper because he peed in the corner (don't worry, I'll deal with this in a minute) he'll soon learn that you coming home is bad news. On the other hand, if he learns that every time he relieves himself in an appropriate location you give him a treat he will anticipate this and want to do it more often. Teaching your pup to build associations between things is the foundation for his learning and throughout this book you'll discover dozens of ways to help him do just that.

In order to effectively build associations…

Your Pup Needs Praise…And Reprimands

In order for your pup to understand that he's done something right he needs you to let him know you're pleased. The best way to do this is through *positive reinforcement*, that is, some kind of pleasurable feedback that he'd like to see happen again. There are three ways in which you can positively reinforce a pup and which you choose will depend on both what most motivates your pup and what's available at the moment you want to reinforce him.

The first way to positively reinforce your puppy is with your voice and physical affection. "That's a good puppy" in an upbeat tone accompanied by some soothing stroking will be hard for him to misinterpret. The sudden appearance of a favorite toy is another powerful motivator for

That's a good puppy!

playful young pups. And finally, a delicious treat is a wonderful way to highlight the moment he did something right. The operant phrase in that last sentence is "the moment he did something right." Of course, I'm speaking about timing. It's important that you positively reinforce your pup at the absolute moment that he does whatever it is that you would like to reinforce him for. Keep in mind, your pup lives utterly in the moment. He will believe that he's being reinforced for whatever it is that he's doing when the praise, treat, or toy shows up.

TOO MUCH OF A GOOD THING

As far as your motivators are concerned please keep in mind that they are motivators for your pup only so long as he values them. To the degree that he has excessive or even unlimited access to your positive reinforcers, to that same degree he might cease to value them.

As far as your motivators are concerned please keep in mind that they are motivators for your pup *only so long as he values them.* To the degree that he has excessive or even unlimited access to your positive reinforcers, to that same degree he might cease to value them. For example, if you're lavishing praise and physical affection on your puppy day and night for no reason whatsoever the value of such praise as positive reinforcement will be diminished. If your pup has his favorite toys strewn all over the place and available at all times their motivating power will be similarly compromised. Do not lavish your pup with everything all at once. Limiting and making conditional his access to whatever motivates him most will do wonders in making him responsive to you. That having been said, be sure to look for as many opportunities to positively reinforce your pup as possible. Too many people notice their pup only when he's doing something undesirable (more on that in a moment) and completely ignore him when he's showing undeniable signs of genius. Since the former is a guaranteed part of puppy ownership please make an extra effort to notice and reinforce the latter. In other words, *catch your pup doing something right and reinforce it as often as possible.*

This brings me to the next subject, the other side of the coin, if you will. Of course I'm referring to reprimands.

Now, this is a touchy subject. In today's world of political correctness there is a school of thought which holds that you should never reprimand a pup, that you should never say "no," that you should ignore unwanted behaviors and simply look for their positive opposites to reinforce. For example, proponents of this school would tell you that if your pup is barking incessantly you should simply do nothing until he quiets himself and then give him a treat for his silence.

Personally, such an approach makes no sense to me. Your job as puppy owner is to definitively outline behavior boundaries for your pup and this is most effectively done through well-timed, meaningful reprimands. Your pup needs and is looking for this feedback. Without it he is lost. And the truth is, in a pack situation it would be no different. As young pups begin to push the behavior boundaries in a pack situation they get instant feedback from other pack members. They are reprimanded in a way that is explosive, perfectly timed to the infraction and over as fast as it started. The whole event might last no more than one or two seconds. *No one gets hurt, there is no lingering on reprimands, no holding of grudges,* but the message is loud and clear: don't do that again! Because of such strong and consistent feedback undesirable behaviors in young pups disappear relatively quickly in a pack context. The only reason they tend to linger on in a human context is because of ineffective and inconsistent feedback.

The key thing to understand when it comes to reprimands is that *they are in no way designed to cause pain or physically injure your pup.* Their main intent is to make a huge psychological impact through the elements of surprise and intensity. *The goal here is not to be mean, but meaningful* and this can be easily accomplished with no physical harm to your pup whatso-ever. Shake cans (empty soda cans with five or six pennies in them to create a loud, rattling sound), squirt bottles

That's a bad puppy!

filled with water or taste deterrents designed to be sprayed in the pup's mouth, scruff shakes (grabbing the pup by his jowls, drawing him up to you or rolling him on his back while maintaining piercing eye contact and issuing a firm verbal reprimand), muzzle grabs (similar to a scruff shake except that you're holding the pup's mouth shut) and hands slamming on crates all achieve the desired effect without damaging your puppy in any way. Hitting, kicking, throwing or in any other way actually hurting the pup does not constitute a reprimand, it constitutes abuse and should be avoided at all costs. There will be more discussion of reprimands and how and when to apply them in the sections that follow.

THE IMPORTANCE OF TIMING

If timing was important with respect to praise, it is doubly important with respect to reprimands. Keep in mind that your pup will believe that he is being reprimanded for whatever he is doing at the moment you reprimand him. In other words, never, ever, for any reason reprimand him after the fact. Not only will he not understand why you are so upset, he may come to think that you're crazy as well. Please never forget that any reprimand must be perfectly timed to the infraction it is meant to correct.

With respect to this issue, there are several other items worth mentioning. First, if timing was important with respect to praise, it is doubly important with respect to reprimands. Keep in mind that your pup will believe that he is being reprimanded for *whatever he is doing at the moment you reprimand him.* In other words, never, ever, for any reason reprimand him after the fact. Not only will he not understand why you are so upset, he may come to think that you're crazy as well. The proof of this, of course, is that not only will the undesirable behavior fail to disappear, but your pup will learn to be afraid of you as well. Please never forget that any reprimand must be perfectly timed to the infraction it is meant to correct.

Second, if you're going to use a reprimand be sure to make it meaningful. That is, try to find just that level of intensity that will get the job done the first time around without unduly terrorizing your pup. In other words, try to avoid both over-reprimanding and under-reprimanding. Over-reprimanding is clearly abusive. Yet under-reprimanding, in my view, is equally abusive.

Why? Because not only will you have to issue more reprimands, your pup will also learn that there's always a little wiggle room in your corrections. Finding that level of intensity that gets the job done the first or second time around is the most humane and efficient way to curb unwanted behaviors in your pup.

Finally, I'd like to come back to a point I made a few moments ago, namely being able to shift your tone with your pup in precise accordance with his changing emotional and behavioral states. In other words, you have to be able to be Jekyll and Hyde and switch back and forth between the two both seamlessly and with lightning speed. For example, you may at one moment have to sharply reprimand your pup for some infraction and in the very next breath be able to wildly praise him for doing something right. The more theatrical you can be the easier it will be for your pup to understand what it is you're trying to say.

In the preceding pages I've said a good bit about communication but I have, as yet, failed to point out that in order to make all of this effective…

Your Pup Needs Consistency

I always have to chuckle a little when a client tells me that they're "pretty consistent" with their dog. As I understand it, "pretty consistent" is an oxymoron not unlike "congressional ethics," "military intelligence," or "a little bit pregnant." That is, as I understand it, the word consistent means "absolutely every time." Anything short of that would be "inconsistent" by definition wouldn't it?

The point is that in order to understand in no uncertain terms what is expected of him your pup needs you to be consistent in your demands. If sometimes you permit a behavior and at other times you reprimand it how in the

WHAT ARE EXTINCTION BURSTS?

Extinction burst is a fancy way of saying that sometimes behaviors get worse before they get better. Imagine that every day at five o'clock you go to visit your good friend down the street and one day when you show up and knock on the door, as you have a hundred times in the past, no one answers. What do you do? You knock again, and then perhaps again and this time a little louder. Perhaps you even repeat this routine several more times before finally giving up. That is an extinction burst. If a behavior has always worked in the past to attain a certain result, before you give it up you're most likely going to work it a little harder. Your pup may do the same if he has been pursuing a behavior that has been giving him a positive payoff for some time that you're now attempting to eliminate. Many owners, when they see this, assume that their behavior modification isn't working when exactly the opposite might be true. Stay the course and you're likely to see improvement soon.

world will your pup ever learn what it is you really want? He won't and it won't be his fault.

Most owners fail to grasp the corrosive influence that a lack of consistency has, not only on their pup's training, but also on their relationship with them. If you are inconsistent your pup will translate that to mean that you are untrustworthy. After all, why else would you be so unpredictable in your responses to him?

Consistency also means that all members of your household should be reading off the same page when it comes to establishing behavior boundaries for your pup. In other words, everyone should hold him to the same standard. Failure to do this will at the very least result in a dog that has different standards of behavior for different household members and at worst in a dog that is confused and insecure in relation to his place in your "pack."

The long and the short of it is that the importance of consistency would be difficult to overestimate. Both the pup's mental and emotional well-being and the quality of your relationship with him depend on it.

In addition to your consistency...

Your Pup Needs To Be Set Up To Succeed

When putting together learning situations for your pup, especially in relation to obedience commands, you should take great care to create scenarios that allow your pup to be successful. By setting him up to succeed you help him to develop a positive attitude not only to training but towards his relationship with you as well as life as a whole. In the section on obedience training you will find a whole host of exercises designed specifically with this purpose in mind.

I'm so proud of you!

While it's definitely possible to teach your young pup not only obedience commands, but a great deal more, as you'll see in the pages that follow, you should also keep in mind that...

Your Pup Has A Limited Attention Span

In many ways, when it comes to training exercises and other interactions that are geared to learning, less is more. That is, it's better to have more short sessions, rather than less long ones. While you'll be amazed as you go through this book not only by how much your pup can learn but by how fast he can learn it, please resist the temptation to always see if you can do "just one more."

In learning there is always a point of diminishing returns where more actually becomes less. In other words, your pup could get bored or worse, burned out, on an exercise – a situation you definitely want to avoid. Work him in very short increments and stop your exercises when you feel like he is performing at the maximum level of which he is capable at that particular moment. Doing so will end the training session on a high note and leave the pup eager for more. In relation to being a guest it's often said that "it's better to leave a day early than to stay a day too long." In the same vein, it's always better to end the session before the pup is ready for it to be over than try to do "just one more" and have your pup not only decline in his level of performance but get sick and tired of the whole exercise.

Wrigley, happy and alert after a training session.

Your Pup Needs A Name

Perhaps with everything that I've just covered I've put the cart before the horse just a little. That is, in order to make any of the above work your puppy needs a name. That name will be his tag, his cue that something relevant is about to happen to him, for the rest of his life. So you should start using it as soon as possible.

The easiest way to introduce your pup to his name is to

Your Pup's Name

Your pup's name is one of the most important ways you have of communicating with him. Keep his name special by only using it when you have to. Avoid chanting it at him all day long or soon it will lose its meaning. Use it to praise and communicate and try to leave it at that.

simply say it and give him a treat. Additionally, you should preface or accompany each interaction with your pup with his name, being simultaneously conscious *never to use his name as a reprimand*. Also, be sure not to drone on endlessly with trying to get his attention. "Bosco, Bosco, Bosco…" will only make your pup deaf to this sound not unlike the way we've all become deaf to the sound of car alarms in the distance. If you conscientiously tie your pup's name to events that are relevant to him you'll be amazed at how fast he'll come to recognize it and respond with his attention.

Your Pup Has "Fear Periods"

Between approximately eight and eleven weeks of age and then again at approximately four and a half to five months your pup will go through a so-called fear period. What this means is that any traumatic incident that he experiences during this time will be likely to have a much greater impact on his psyche than if that same incident occurred either before or after this period.

Wh..Whoa! What's that?

During your pup's fear period you'll have to walk a bit of a fine line. On the one hand you want to be sure to shelter him from situations where sudden, intense and unexpected events could rattle his little psyche. On the other hand, as you'll see shortly, you need to vigorously and pro-actively socialize him to all sorts of experiences with which he'll have to live as he grows up. In short, you should exercise caution and discretion during this period while still providing a rich variety of encounters and interactions for your pup.

Your Pup Is Not A Person

You are a person, your pup is a puppy and a puppy is a full-grown dog waiting to happen. While it is true that dogs and humans have a great deal in common, which is, after all, why we get along so well together, there are a great many significant differences which must be taken into account. Your dog, no matter what breed, is essentially a watered down, domesticated wolf, not a diminutive person in a fur coat. While this might seem obvious it's endlessly amazing how many otherwise intelligent human beings fall prey to a tendency known as *anthropomorphism*. Anthropomorphism is a fancy term that basically means attributing human characteristics and motivations to animals, in this case your pup.

The most common manifestations of anthropomorphism are found in statements such as "he looks guilty because he knows he's done something wrong," or "he was angry at me and therefore he put his dirty paws on my white sofa." Attributing such human motivations to your pup can quickly lead you to inappropriate reactions and send your relationship into a downward spiral. Trust me when I tell you that he is not capable of forming Shakespearean plots of revenge against you and if he looks guilty it's because he's afraid of you, not because he's experiencing remorse over something he did two hours ago. While there are many cases where one might be able to make a convincing argument for guilt I promise you there is always another explanation.

The area in which this little piece of information is the most important is in relation to reprimands. Please, no matter what emotions and motivations you are tempted to attribute to your pup, never reprimand him for something he did even just a few seconds ago. Remember, your pup lives in the moment and will assume that he's being reprimanded for whatever he's doing at the moment you reprimand him. That delayed reprimands are always misguided is best evidenced by the fact that they never seem to stop the unwanted behavior. So please resist the sometimes overwhelming temptation to chew him out when he's done something particularly annoying at some point in the past.

HE KNOWS HE'S BEEN BAD

"He looks guilty because he knows he's done something wrong," or "he was angry at me and therefore he put his dirty paws on my white sofa," the distraught owner often says. Trust me when I tell you that your pup is not capable of forming Shakespearean plots of revenge against you and if he looks guilty it's because he's afraid of you, not because he's experiencing remorse over something he did two hours ago.

Finally, Your Pup Needs Love!

By love I don't mean some sweet, sentimental and syrupy emotion but a great and heartfelt caring for the welfare of your pup. It is this caring that will give you the patience and attention necessary to pull together everything I've mentioned so far and set aside, when necessary, your own impulses. It will allow you to channel your love to your pup in such a way as to forge a deep and profound bond between the two of you, one that will last for many years and enrich both of your lives.

That having been said, let's turn our attention to the more functional issues of raising a puppy beginning with what most people consider the most pressing (no pun intended) – housebreaking.

Photos: Carol Irvine, Irvine Photo

Love and...

Kisses!

THE THREE PILLARS OF HOUSEBREAKING

INTRODUCTION

Often it seems that a pup is little more than a pooping and peeing machine. Every time you turn around you find a new puddle or pile in the wake of your happy go lucky fur ball. The unavoidable fact is that messes in the house are simply a part of puppy ownership. A young pup has practically no bladder or bowel control and he's consuming food at an enormous rate in relation to his tiny digestive system in order to meet the nutritional demands of his body's growth. So the real question isn't: "are you going to have accidents in the house?" it's "for how long will they go on?" If you keep a few simple principles in mind you should be able to eliminate accidents in the house in relatively short order.

Not in my shoe, please!

The trick to housebreaking can be summed up in three magic words: *confine, supervise and regulate.* Remember and apply them and you'll be on your way shortly. In practical terms what this means is that if your dog is not confined he should be supervised, if he can't be supervised he should be confined and the structure of his day should be regulated so that as much as possible his routine is identical from day to day. Remember, dogs crave structure. Intelligently combining these three elements will quickly give your pup the information he needs to eliminate inappropriate elimination sooner rather than later. Below I will outline the general contours of a solid housebreaking program and then I'll discuss variations that can be made to that program in order to adapt it to the needs of your lifestyle. With that let's take a look at the first pillar.

OTHER REASONS TO CRATE TRAIN

Aside from housebreaking there are numerous other good reasons to acclimate your pup to a crate as early as possible. Consider, for instance, that if you ever wish to fly your dog anywhere – he will be crated. If you ever have to leave him at the vet overnight – he will be crated. If you're driving him around in the car he's the safest when – he's crated. If he's ever going to board at a professional boarding facility, even if he's out all day playing, at night – he will be crated. The fact is that there are numerous situations that require your dog to be crated so why not introduce the whole idea early on, during his critical socializing period, while his whole relationship to life is so malleable? In this way the dog will always view his crate as a safe haven, a comfort zone, even when all the other elements of his environment change radically such as in the examples mentioned above.

A crate, properly introduced, becomes a doggie condo.

Confine

The most important thing to understand when speaking of confinement is that *dogs, by nature, are den animals.* That is, they like the comfort and security of small, confined spaces. If you've had dogs in the past you might have noticed that they often like to hang around under coffee tables, beds and in tight corners. It's natural for dogs to seek such places of shelter because they offer maximum safety and protection. In other words, they are very den-like. Because of this the most effective tool for confining a pup is a *crate* (that's doggie for den or canine for condo) and, when properly introduced, is it not only *not* cruel but might well become your pup's favorite hang-out.

In relation to housebreaking crates are important because they take advantage of the pup's strong *nesting instinct.* That is, dogs have a powerful habit of keeping their den clean because, just like humans, they have a natural aversion to being near their own messes. In fact, they like to be as far away from them as possible and they definitely don't want them in their den. Crating takes advantage of this instinct by providing maximum incentive for your pup to exercise whatever level of self-control he has. No puppy wants to eliminate in his crate. Thus, if you are diligent in getting him out at regular intervals, as you will see in a moment, accidents in the house should disappear relatively quickly.

Ideally you'll have a crate ready when you bring your new puppy home so you can begin to acclimate him to it immediately. Most typically your puppy will begin to bark, scream, whine and complain and generally throw a fit the first few times you put him in there and lock the door. This is to be expected. After all, for all of his young life he has been continually surrounded by and nestled in with mom and his littermates, a warm, fuzzy and intimately familiar situation. Then suddenly you came along, plucked him from his comfortable and cozy surroundings and expect him to sleep alone in his new den. Understandably, this is all a bit traumatic for your pup. It will take him a little time to adjust to his new situation and adopt you as his intimately familiar companion.

Thankfully, there is a great deal you can do to help him. Outfitting the crate for maximum comfort is the first step. Lots of soft, fuzzy bedding is a great place to start (some of the cold weather breeds may not care for this but most dogs will). While it's not a replacement for mom and siblings it should mimic the warm and cushy

WHAT'S YOUR PLEASURE?

Crates basically come in two varieties, wire mesh and plastic. Wire mesh is good for hot climates and areas and they fold down easily. Plastic crates are usually accepted for airline travel and are a little warmer and cozier. Either is fine.

Photos: Mike Wombacher

surroundings still so fresh in the young pup's mind. To make the situation even more comforting on cool nights I usually put a hot water bottle under the bedding, the warmth of which will seep throughout the crate and the pup's body and often lull him to sleep. To sweeten the deal even more I'll sprinkle a handful of treats inside the crate, which the pup will usually have a fun time finding by nosing his way through the bedding. A Kong Toy (a hard rubber toy, odd shaped and hollow) stuffed with peanut butter or cheese wouldn't hurt either. One final little trick that can also help is to take an old fashioned ticking alarm clock, wrap it in towel and set it in a corner of the crate. The rhythm of the ticking can have a hypnotic and comforting effect on your pup much as the sound of his mother's heartbeat used to.

Now, despite the fact that you're holding up your end by making the crate as comfy as possible it's still possible that at some point your pup will throw a tantrum and demand to be let out. If you haven't read the section on reprimands (p.33) now might be a good time to do so because it's at this point that you must give him some information about the dim view you take of this behavior. Of course, since you view this behavior in less than a positive light *the absolute worst possible thing you could do is give in to the pup's barking and crying and let him out.* Just doing this once will likely make the behavior skyrocket as the pup has now hit upon a strategy that gets results. What's worse, this discovery can quickly bleed over into all other aspects of his relationship with you as the "I scream, I get" outlook on life takes him over like a bad fungus.

So what is the best way to respond? By giving your pup some dramatic negative feedback about his behavior. This could include such measures as slamming your hand on his crate loudly while commanding "quiet," lobbing a shake can (an empty soda can with five or six pennies in

it) from a hidden location at the crate the instant the barking begins, or using a squirt bottle filled either with water or a taste deterrent such as Bitter Apple spray or Binaca breath spray to squirt the pup squarely in the nose and mouth area accompanied by the command "quiet." The latter is my favorite as I've found it the least jarring and most effective with young pups. Now, to more sensitive readers this might seem harsh and inappropriate but keep in mind what I said above about reprimands (see p.33). The idea, once again, is not to be mean, but meaningful. *These reprimands do not hurt the pup but send a sudden, loud and clear message.*

If you are persistent in your reprimands while at the same time continuing to make the crate inviting the way I suggested above, your pup will sooner or later (some pups are quite persistent) figure "hey, if I throw a fit they scream, throw shake cans and spray me, but if I just settle down I can chew on my toy, dig around for treats and enjoy the warmth of my den." Rocket science isn't a prerequisite for your pup to figure this out.

Another question that often arises in relation to crates is how long you can reasonably expect the pup to stay in one without having to go to the bathroom. While every pup is different, and you'll need to observe your own pup to figure this out, the best rule of thumb I've ever run across is as many hours as he is months old, plus one. For example, if he's two months old three hours are probably okay. That having been said, I personally never like to crate a dog, pup or adult, for more than four hours during the daytime without some kind of outing, either for elimination or exercise, except in extreme circumstances.

All of the above having been said, it should be clear that the purpose of crating is to give your pup maximum incentive to contain himself. However, this doesn't mean

LEAVING YOUR PUP FOR LONGER PERIODS OF TIME

If you're going to have to leave your pup for a longer time than it's appropriate to crate him - about three to four hours - then use a collapsible ex-pen to create a confined area for him. You can put his crate in the enclosed area with the door open and put papers down over the whole area in the likely event that your pup will eliminate, (see photos, pp. 60 - 61).

he will do so forever. After all, when you've gotta go, you've gotta go. Nowhere is this more true than with young puppies. Thus, your job as owner is *to be sure that your pup is outside in an area you have deemed appropriate for his toilet activities when he needs to go.* Since initially you don't know when he needs to go it's good policy to take him out every hour or so until you see a pattern emerging. Does this mean that your pup is to always be in his crate unless he is eliminating? Of course not! That would be extraordinarily inhumane and brings us to the second pillar of our housebreaking program.

Supervise

Clearly your pup can't be expected to spend his entire life in the crate or in his potty area. He needs to have ample time to explore his surroundings, play with you and otherwise entertain himself. However, he is only to have opportunity for such activity *under your strict supervision.* You wouldn't let a two year old child just wander around your house without keeping an eye on him so don't do it with your pup either. In short, *your pup should never have any unsupervised activity around your house during his critical socialization period.* Not only would such activity have seriously detrimental effects on your housebreaking program, it would allow your pup to get into all sorts of trouble without you being in a position to reprimand him (see p.99 and appendix for common household dangers). In the context of housebreaking supervision enables you to do two things. First, it allows you to observe your pup for signs of needing to eliminate and second, it allows you to give him important feedback about eliminating in places you don't want him to. Let's take a look at each of those in turn.

Supervision is the key to both housebreaking and house manners.

First, puppies generally need to eliminate on three

occasions: *after waking*, even if only from a short nap; *after eating* or drinking; and *during or immediately after vigorous play*. You can easily tell when a pup's mind is preoccupied with the need to relieve himself. Generally he'll stop whatever he's doing and begin sniffing around a bit anxiously as if he's lost his keys. When he starts doing that you'd better scoop him up and get him outside to his designated area. Once he's eliminated you can bring him back inside and allow him to play as he was before. On the other hand, if you've taken him outside and he hasn't eliminated, having gotten sidetracked with all the interesting smells and sounds of the great outdoors, you should definitely *not* bring him back into the house and play with him or he'll almost certainly pee or poop where you'd rather he didn't. Instead, you should return him to his crate, give him fifteen minutes of down time and then take him out to his potty area once more. This will allow the need to eliminate to rise to the surface of his consciousness once more and will increase your likelihood of success the second time around. If he once again fails to eliminate simply repeat the procedure. Only when he has eliminated would you allow him to spend more time freewheeling in your house – with your supervision, of course. In relation to this, it's not necessary to stand with the pup in his elimination area forever waiting for him to do something. After four or five minutes bring him back inside, confine him, and try him a little later.

Between the two pillars discussed so far, confinement and supervision, your pup should simply have no opportunities to eliminate inappropriately

THE PUPPY UMBILICAL CORD

A great way to both confine and supervise your pup simultaneously while freely moving about your house is to simply tie him to yourself (see p.148 for leash training) and have him follow you around. Along the same lines, if you're spending some time say, cooking in the kitchen or working at your computer, you can simply tie the pup up nearby and give him a chew bone to amuse himself. In this way he doesn't have to be constantly confined to his crate or play area if you're not actively supervising him and he can begin to be exposed to the rest of your house and learn to participate in a larger chunk of your life.

A secondary benefit of this approach to supervision is that it teaches your pup that his entire life is determined by your actions. If you move, he has to move with you. If you're quietly hanging around he has to do the same. In short, it teaches him from the earliest times to get in the habit of taking direction from you rather than having endless opportunities to make his own decisions, decisions which will most likely get him into trouble.

CLEANING UP DOGGIE MESSES

If your pup has eliminated in the house you'll need to clean the spot with an enzymatic cleaner such as Nature's Miracle™ or Dr. Foster and Smith's Dogtergent™. These products are specifically designed to remove the smells that attract pups back to the same spot to eliminate again and will help your floors and carpets survive the travails of puppyhood.

If your pup eliminates outside there are several ways to clean it up. The simplest and most common way is to take a plastic bag, such as the one's you get your groceries in, put your hand inside it as if it were a glove, reach down, pick up the mess, and turn the bag inside out, trapping the foul deposit. Then you can simply tie off the bag and throw it in the trash.

Another, more environmentally conscious way to dispose of dog messes, is to use one of the waste disposal systems that can be installed in your backyard. Generally these involve digging a hole into which a disposal system is buried. Once buried you simply drop all doggie waste into it and once a week or so add a harmless chemical that helps to break the waste down and allows it to be absorbed into the soil. Generally systems like this can be ordered from catalogs such as Drs. Foster and Smith (800-981-7179 or www.drsfostersmith.com).

without being observed. However, there will definitely be times when he will eliminate shamelessly right in front of you. As I've already mentioned, this is to be expected as he has essentially no bladder or bowel control. However, because you're supervising him you're in a position to give him some feedback about this behavior. If you see your pup squat to poop or to pee loudly clap your hands to interrupt him and *with a voice filled with urgency – not anger –* say "no," or "ah ah ah," run over, scoop him up, take him out to his area to eliminate and praise him like crazy if he does. If he doesn't, simply return him to his crate and try him again about ten to fifteen minutes later. Soon he'll realize that eliminating inside gets you frantic and eliminating outside makes you happy and this understanding will begin to set him on the right road.

In this context it's important to understand that you should *never harshly punish a puppy for eliminating in the wrong area.* You definitely should not rub his nose in it, hit him with a rolled up newspaper, tie him up next to it, or even scream angrily at him for his faux pas. Doing any of these things simply teaches your pup that you, he, and a pile or a puddle in the same place are a bad idea. The next logical conclusion for him is to never go to the bathroom in front of you but rather to hide and find out of the way places to eliminate. Again, simply startle him with a loud handclap – this will often stop the pup in his tracks – use an urgent tone as you scoop him up and bring him to where you'd like him to eliminate. My experience with my own pup was that after I was able to catch her, take her out and actually have her finish outside three times, she simply got it. I could almost see the little light bulb go off over her head as she realized "oh, not here, there." While every pup is different, catching them, interrupting them and encouraging them to finish outside can be key to nailing the concept down in their minds.

As a corollary, of course, if you find a pile or a puddle that you did not see happen and you feel the need to reprimand someone please reprimand yourself. The only way such a thing could happen is if you weren't as diligent in your supervision as you should have been. Such incidents are also an almost inevitable part of housebreaking but will serve to show you where the holes in your system are and thus allow you to patch them. So you see, even you're not too old to learn a new trick now and again.

Now, on to pillar number three.

Regulate

Putting your puppy on a routine and regimenting his little life as much as possible is also extremely helpful in house-breaking. As I mentioned above (p.26), dogs are creatures of habit. The more they are made to follow a strict routine the more their little bodies and minds adapt to it and the more they come to expect it. This type of regularity is very com-forting and makes your pup feel that life is safe, secure and predictable.

Keeping to a tight schedule is key to housebreaking.

In relation to housebreaking you want to regulate both feeding times and elimination times. Most owners feed very young puppies three times a day. That's fine. Just try and be sure that it's always more or less the same time. Regular inputs tend to produce regular outputs. Please do not free feed your dog, that is, leave food out for him all day long. If your pup nibbles at his food here and there it will be much more difficult for you to tell when he's going to need to go to the bathroom. At feeding times put his food down for ten to fifteen minutes and whatever he hasn't eaten, throw it back in the bag. He'll see it again at the next mealtime. If your pup is particular and turns his nose up at his food that's fine. He'll be hungrier the next time around and will soon figure out that he's got specific windows of opportunity to eat and that he should take advantage of them. Trust me, he won't starve himself.

As far as elimination is concerned, in the early days your pup will seemingly need to go without rhyme or reason. During this time you should take him out every hour or so, if possible. Soon, however, you'll begin to see a pattern emerge and you should try to align yourself with that. In other words, be sure he's out when he needs to be out. For example, if you know that he's usually got to go ten minutes after his mealtimes try to always take him out at those times. Also, keep in mind that he will most likely need to go immediately after waking and after only a few short minutes of vigorous play. At any rate, try to observe his rhythms and get in sync with them. As he gets older you'll be able to make adjustments to his routine based on your needs but in order to eliminate accidents in the house as soon as possible with a very young pup you need to work in accordance with his needs more than your own.

By getting in sync and establishing a routine your pup will come to not only expect but depend on this regularity and will derive great peace of mind from it. For example, if, as your pup gets older, he consistently learns when his bathroom time is, he'll have no reason to be anxious about anything. He'll know that "fifteen more minutes and I get

THREE KEY TIMES FOR ELIMINATION

Your pup will tend to need to eliminate on three occasions. First, after waking. Second, after eating or drinking and third, during vigorous play.

Pay extra attention at these times and be sure to get him out!

to go out and go potty" and will, *as he gets older,* work to restrain himself until the appointed time. He won't have to worry "Oh my God, I've got to go. When are they going to take me out?" He'll come to know his time is just around the corner and breathe easier in that knowledge. And frankly, wouldn't you?

Pulling It All Together

Now that we've examined the three pillars of housebreaking let's take a look at how they work together to support your housebreaking program on a day-to-day basis. Of course, the routine outlined below is only a blueprint – one in which I've tried to address common problems as well – and you'll have to work out the details of your own schedule based on the necessities of your life. Nonetheless, I hope you will find it helpful. So without further adieu, let's dive in.

First thing in the morning, gather your senses and take your pup out to an area you have designated as the doggie bathroom. With very young pups it's best to simply pick them up and take them out rather than letting them follow you out since they'll be bursting and will often stop halfway to the door and relieve themselves. It's also a good idea to have a leash (see p.148 for teaching your puppy to wear a leash) on your pup so once outside you can restrict him to a particular area and help define this area as the bathroom. Otherwise pups have a tendency to roam about looking for new and interesting places to eliminate and, before you know it, your backyard has become more treacherous than a Cambodian minefield. A five-foot by five-foot area should be sufficient and if you're feeling particularly generous you could find a second spot as well. After all, who doesn't like having two bathrooms in the house? Once you've gotten your pup out, set him down in the designated area and let him sniff about. If he begins to wander out of the designated zone bring him back into it with very gentle nudges on the leash. (If you bring him to the same spot consistently he'll soon choose to eliminate there on his own.)

ELIMINATING ON COMMAND

As esoteric as this might sound, it's an extraordinarily simple thing to accomplish. Simply find a suitable phrase such as "get busy" or "hurry up" and gently repeat it over and over again to the pup while he's eliminating, not before and not after, but during the act. The moment your pup is done reward him with a little treat which you have thoughtfully brought along to celebrate the occasion. This teaches him to associate his body action (eliminating) with a sound ("hurry up") and a positive result at the end (a treat).

Since it's morning time it shouldn't take him too long to find a spot and unburden himself. While he is eliminating (either #1 or #2) you have a wonderful opportunity to teach him to do this on command. As esoteric as this might sound, it's an extraordinarily simple thing to accomplish. Simply find a suitable phrase such as "get busy" or "hurry up" and gently repeat it over and over again to the pup while he's eliminating, *not before and not after, but during the act.* The moment your pup is done reward him with a little treat which you have thoughtfully brought along to celebrate the occasion. This teaches him to associate his body action (eliminating) with a sound ("hurry up") and a positive result at the end (a treat). Repeat this procedure both after urinating and defecating and do it consistently. You'll be amazed how fast your pup will begin to respond to your request to eliminate.

Once your dog is done eliminating clean up any messes right then and there if possible. It's important, if you want your dog to return to the same spot repeatedly, to keep the area reasonably clean. Dogs, despite the nasty things they sometimes get into, are relatively clean animals. They will avoid eliminating in an area that still has evidence from the last outing lying there by choosing a spot a bit further away. If the next time the two offending items are still there he will find a third spot and so forth and so on. Before you know it you're in the minefield scenario once again. Keep the area clean and you won't have these problems.

Now that you've taken your pup out to the bathroom, rewarded him, and brought him back inside it's time for breakfast. Remember, no free feeding. Put his dish down for fifteen minutes or so and throw whatever he hasn't eaten back in the bag. After breakfast you'll have to keep a close eye on him since, as I told you a few moments ago, pups tend to eliminate on three occasions, one of which is after eating. So now you're back in the danger zone. How long after eating it takes for a pup to need to eliminate varies but

ON THE LIGHTER SIDE...

Ever wonder what your dog's thinking? I saw a hysterical cartoon the other day that depicted a dog owner dutifully picking up her canine's fecal deposit with her hand in a plastic bag, a chore most dog owners are intimately familiar with. Behind her her dog is watching with a puzzled expression on his face. The little bubble over his head reveals his thoughts: "my God, man. Just sniff it and be done with it. Why save it?"

fifteen to thirty minutes is about average. If you play with him for a little while after breakfast you'll quickly meet the second elimination criteria: during or after vigorous play which means you'll have to keep an extra close eye on him. Again, if he starts looking around as if he's lost his keys you should get him out – fast. Once outside simply repeat the procedure outlined above.

Muffin, the Maltese is in good hands.

It's possible at this point, or at any point for that matter, that your pup might have a little surprise in store for you: failure to cooperate. In other words, now that he's all worked up from his playtime and with all the distractions outside, it might not occur to him to take a break from all that fun in order to eliminate even if he has too. He just wants to keep playing. What many owners end up doing is continuing to engage their pup in play once in the potty area or stand around for twenty minutes waiting for the pup to deliver the goods. Once the pup does finally perform he is immediately brought inside because all the owner ever wanted was for him to eliminate. Big mistake! *Always separate playtime from time potty time.* In other words, if you're going out in order to have your pup eliminate do not play with him unless it's *after* he's done the deed. Otherwise your pup learns that the longer he *doesn't* go the longer he gets to play and conversely, when he does go the fun is over. Pups are smarter than you think. Which do you think he'll choose?

Additionally, do not stand out there with him and wait around forever. Teach him that he has a window of opportunity to eliminate. How big should that window be? My personal standard is about the length of time it takes for a commercial break to run during my favorite television program or about three to four minutes. If your pup does not eliminate during this timeframe bring him back inside and crate him for about ten to fifteen minutes or until the next commercial break. Then try him again. If

Courtesy: Mary Watson

Woody is curious and polite - a model standard poodle pup.

he fails to eliminate again repeat the procedure. Promptly returning your pup to his crate when he doesn't eliminate outside prevents him from coming back in where the stimulation level is lower and suddenly remembering his need to go. Only when he finally does deliver the goods outside can you give him some *supervised* freedom inside.

Throughout the day continue with this routine or some semblance thereof. Feed, play, eliminate, play some more, crate awhile, eliminate, play, feed, eliminate, crate, etc. Remember that you can use the umbilical cord and tie down approaches (see p.49) to both confine and supervise your pup during the course of your day. Also, bear in mind that keeping whatever routine you establish consistent from day to day will be extraordinarily helpful to your pup.

As you approach evening time be sure to take up your pup's food and water at least three hours before bedtime and give him minimally two more opportunities to eliminate before putting him to bed. This will ensure that he is as empty as possible before bedtime and it will help you get him through the night. However, sometimes, with a very young pup, you're going to need to bite the bullet and take him out in the middle of the night in order to avoid him eliminating in his crate.

In this connection, I would not recommend just gating your pup in some small part of the house such as a bathroom and allowing him to eliminate there at night primarily because this can teach him that sometimes it's actually okay to eliminate inside and thus fail to develop the discipline to contain himself until you get him out. While there are circumstances that might demand such an approach (more on that shortly) I would encourage you to avoid this if at all possible.

Instead, try the following routine. First, put your crate next to your bed so you can hear your pup and determine if he needs to go out. Additionally, place a spray bottle filled with water or a taste deterrent (see pp.80-81) on top of the crate so you can reprimand him for unnecessary barking (see p.96). Having the crate next to you allows you to both monitor the pup and reprimand him if necessary without having to leave your bed. It also serves to give the young pup the comfort and security of knowing someone is there in lieu of mom and littermates. This will tend to help him sleep more comfortably in the early stages. For those of you who don't want your pup in the bedroom, fear not. It's not a difficult matter once he is sleeping through the night and comfortable with his new pack, to move him out of the bedroom. But in the beginning it's just a much easier way to go for all concerned.

Now, there are two approaches you can use to get through the night. The first involves getting up in about three hour increments and taking your pup out. Follow the elimination routine outlined above. Once your pup is finished promptly return him to his crate. *Never play with your puppy in the middle of the night!* Nighttime is not playtime. It's sleep time. Do not teach your pup to demand play sessions in the dead of night or he'll come to expect them and end up driving you crazy. Once your pup is back in bed he should be expected to settle down and go back to sleep. If he barks and complains reprimand him as described in the section on crate training (pp.46-47). Be consistent and relentless. Teach him that barking and complaining in the crate is simply not an option. It shouldn't be too difficult for him if he's learned this during the daytime already. Soon you'll find that he gets the idea and goes right back to sleep once he's settled back into his crate.

The other approach you can take at night is to simply wait until you hear the pup whining a bit because he needs to eliminate and take him out then. Now by doing this you are technically breaking one of the rules – never let him

IN THE BEDROOM

During the first few weeks with your new pup it's best to have his crate in your bedroom next to your bed. Your pup will derive a great sense of comfort from this, making his transition into your life easier, and it allows you to monitor him without leaving your bed. Once your pup is housebroken and has settled into his new life you can ease him out of the bedroom if you wish.

A tight fit, but manageable.

out when he's complaining – but handled properly this shouldn't be a big problem. If you hear your puppy express his discomfort upon waking give him the benefit of the doubt and get him out. Once he's eliminated immediately return him to bed. Now, if he complains after he's been returned, reprimand him. Soon he'll understand the concept – complaining for any other reason than the need for elimination leads to a correction.

These nocturnal excursions with your pup may, in the beginning, occur as often as three times nightly. However, as he grows even a little older you should be able to drop these little outings one by one and by the time he's three to three and a half months of age he should be able to sleep through the night without needing to eliminate. This effort will be well worth it as your pup will be strengthening his habit of going to the bathroom outside, a habit which he will soon have internalized permanently.

Following a routine such as the one I have outlined above should lead to accident free puppy ownership relatively quickly. However, *this does not mean that your pup is necessarily housetrained.* It only means you're doing a good job confining, supervising and regulating him. But, given the opportunity your pup might still eliminate in the house. The two benchmarks I use to determine if a dog is reliably housetrained are that he should be six to eight months of age *and* have not had an accident in the house for at least two months. Of course, your two-month count always begins again at the time of the most recent accident but once you've reached this goal you can breathe a little easier regarding your pup's bathroom habits.

One final thought in regard to this. If you feel that your pup has been doing really well on his housebreaking and he's having a sudden reversion there may be a health problem such as a bladder or urinary tract infection, in which case all bets are off. Your pup simply can't help himself. Be patient, get him to the vet and be prepared to go back to square one temporarily. What you'll find is that once he's healthy again he'll quickly progress right to where

When Can I Trust Him?

There are two benchmarks to attain before your pup should be considered reliably houebroken. First, he should be between six to eight months of age and second, he should have had no accidents in the house for at least two months.

he was before he fell ill, *if you've gone back to square one* and gotten him out very diligently during his illness.

The information outlined above should give you everything you need to efficiently housebreak your puppy. Of course, it makes the major assumption that someone is home all day and has the time available to be as diligent as this program demands, an assumption that may be altogether wrong. In the next section I'll discuss other approaches and problem solving tools in relation to housebreaking but before doing so I'd like to summarize what I've covered so far.

1. The Three Pillars

    a. **Confine**

        i. Use a crate.

        ii. Make it inviting

        iii. Reprimand complaining

        iv. If he's not confined…

    b. **Supervise**

        i. Use umbilical cord and tie down approach when possible.

        ii. If he's not supervised, confine.

    c. **Regulate**

        i. Get him out on regular intervals.

        ii. If you feel he should have to go and he doesn't return him to confinement for a short period and try him again. Do not allow him to wander around until he's eliminated.

    d. **Other Elements**

        i. Do not use harsh reprimands if you see your pup eliminating inappropriately.

KEEP AN EYE ON HIS HEALTH

If you're experiencing great difficulty or sudden reversions in housebreaking despite following these instructions diligently your pup might have a health issue.

Urinary tract and bladder infections as well as vaginitis, worms and giardia can make housebreaking impossible. Continual leaking or dribbling are signs of potential health problems as well.

In addition, any sudden changes in your pup's behavior should be monitored as indicators of health. For instance, has he suddenly lost his appetite or found one that wasn't there before? Is he listless when he's usually active? Is he consuming abnormally large quantities of water? Does he drag his rear end along the ground when he's sitting? Does he have a thick discharge from his nose or eyes? Is there a funky odor wafting from his ears? If so, take a ride to the vet and see what's up!

ii.   Never reprimand him after the fact.

iii. Never play with him during any bathroom outing. Stick to the business at hand.

iv.   Keep his bathroom area clean.

v.   Teach him to go to the bathroom on command.

vi.   Take him out at regular intervals at night until he can make all the way through without needing to eliminate.

vii. Never play with him at night.

viii. Do not consider your pup housebroken until:

a.   He's six to eight months of age and

b.   Hasn't had any accidents in the house for two months.

Owner Absent Housebreaking or What If I'm Out Earning a Living?

As I mentioned a moment ago, the program I have just described makes the very big assumption that you are home a better part of the day and are able to make this highly regimented routine happen. I understand that this often is not the case and that there are circumstances that can complicate the effort to establish a solid housebreaking routine. If you are forced to be away from home most of the day you'll need to use a different approach to housetraining.

A functional ex-pen set-up. A tarp underneath, papers on top, a bed in the back.

Begin by finding a small area where you can confine your pup during the day. This area should be large enough to contain his crate, water dish, toys and an area to play in. You can create such an area in a number of ways. Begin by simply picking a room, such as the kitchen, which has a hardwood, tile or linoleum floor and cordon it off from the rest of your house by closing the doors or using baby gates. You can section off a piece of hallway using baby gates or something called an "expen" (short for exercise pen), a collapsible folding metal or plastic enclosure, to create a play area for the dog. Try, if possible, not to lock the pup in a small room such as a bathroom by closing the door. This can make him feel visually cut off from the rest of your house and thus imprisoned. A baby gate or ex-pen allows your puppy visual access to a greater area and diminishes his sense of being trapped while a closed door often does exactly the opposite.

Whatever approach to confinement you use, in the beginning be sure to cover the entire area available to the pup with newspapers. Not only will this make it easy for you to clean up the mess, it will begin to habituate the pup to going on the papers. At first you'll find that the pup will randomly eliminate all over the place without any seeming rhyme or reason. Not only that, he will most likely also derive a great deal of pleasure from tearing apart all the carefully laid out newspapers with the efficiency of a White House paper shredder. To prevent this try taping the edges of the paper down with masking tape or spraying them with Bitter Apple spray (he won't smell it, but he'll taste it). If he still shreds them, don't worry about it. Sometimes that's just part of it. What you will also find, however, is that as the days and weeks wear on your pup will begin to show a preference for certain areas in which to eliminate. When this begins to happen you can start reducing the amount of paper you put in his enclosure, covering the floor only around the areas where the pup has shown an inclination to do his business. Do this in small increments, slowly reducing the size of the covered area. If you find that your pup starts peeing next to the papers you've gone too fast and should again increase the coverage accordingly. You can also put a slightly soiled paper under the fresh paper in the

Here the papers have been reduced to one corner and the pup is well on its way.

Photos: Mike Wombacher

And that's Lilly at home in her bed.

middle to draw the pup onto the paper. Be sure to clean the floor well because the urine could seep to the edge causing him to go there. Sooner or later you will find that your pup starts targeting the papers systematically and will likely even seek them out when he is not confined to his play area.

If you have a small dog and your goal is simply to paper-train him in the house your job is more or less done. Of course you'll still have to follow the rules of housebreaking outlined above, i.e., confine, supervise, and regulate, making sure you get your pup to the papers when he needs to go while you're home until you've attained your housebreaking benchmarks (see p.58) but essentially, you're home free.

However, if your goal is to ultimately have him eliminate outside and wean him off the papers, there's more to do. Begin by moving the papers closer to the door in very small increments, perhaps just an inch a day. If your puppy is suddenly missing the papers move them back to the previous spot and keep working from there. The goal, of course, is to ultimately get the papers outside and teach your pup to begin eliminating there. Once he is used to this you'll be able to remove the papers and your pup will be well on his way to being house trained. This will become increasingly easy for him to do as he gets older and attains greater bladder and bowel control. Again, confine, supervise and regulate until your housebreaking benchmarks have been satisfied.

Of course, if your dog is confined for eight hours a day – something I don't recommend as a steady diet – then weaning him off the papers can be rather difficult since he'll be so habituated to going on them that he'll have no incentive to stop even when other alternatives are available. If your life situation prevents you from getting your dog out you should, as he gets older (definitely no sooner than the end of his inoculations), consider getting him a mid-day

HELPING HIM FIND HIS WAY

One helpful trick in getting your pup to find his way to the papers is this: when your pup wakes up take him to some part of the house and then walk him over to his papers, saying "papers" and reward once he eliminates. This will teach him to find the spot from various parts of the house on his own very quickly.

dog walker. Not only will he get much needed exercise and stimulation this way, he'll also have the opportunity to relieve himself at approximately four hour intervals and this, of course, will be tremendously helpful in your efforts at housebreaking. Once the mid-day outing is a part of his routine you can try to reduce the size of his indoor area significantly thus giving him the incentive, due to his nesting instinct, to contain himself. This shouldn't be too difficult if he's had vigorous exercise during his outing since he'll most likely fall asleep until you come home and take him out.

Create a pen or push the crate up to the doggie door (take the crate door out first) and...

A Doggie Door and the Self Training Pup

The biggest problem with paper training, and the reason that I seek to avoid in all but the most necessary situations, is that it teaches the pup not just to use the papers *but to eliminate in the house.* For this reason, if the goal is to ultimately get the pup outside to eliminate, I am always looking for different approaches to accomplishing this based both on the owner's schedule and the layout of the home.

One of the most useful housetraining aids for the "owner-absent" puppy is a doggie door. If you have a deck or a yard of any kind a doggie door can help teach your pup to eliminate outside even if you're not there. Here's how to set it up. Take a crate, remove it's door and put it up to the doggie door so that its opening fits around the entirety of the doggie door. Then put something heavy behind the crate to ensure that it stays firmly wedged up against the opening no matter what your pup is doing inside. On the other side of the doggie door, the outdoor side, put an ex-pen or some other enclosure that is arranged such that once the pup is outside he'll automatically find himself within its confines – a sizeable area within which he can relieve himself. I have had excellent results with this approach since your

on the other side have some kind of enclosure. Presto! Instant housebreaking.

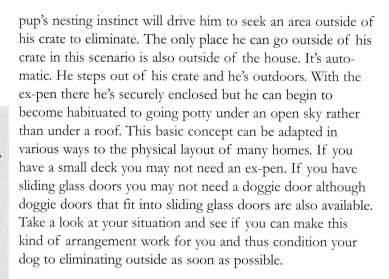

pup's nesting instinct will drive him to seek an area outside of his crate to eliminate. The only place he can go outside of his crate in this scenario is also outside of the house. It's automatic. He steps out of his crate and he's outdoors. With the ex-pen there he's securely enclosed but he can begin to become habituated to going potty under an open sky rather than under a roof. This basic concept can be adapted in various ways to the physical layout of many homes. If you have a small deck you may not need an ex-pen. If you have sliding glass doors you may not need a doggie door although doggie doors that fit into sliding glass doors are also available. Take a look at your situation and see if you can make this kind of arrangement work for you and thus condition your dog to eliminating outside as soon as possible.

Before going further I'd like to summarize the alternatives outlined above.

Summary

1. Enclose your pup in an area with a non-porous surface such as linoleum, tile or hardwood.

2. Cover the entire area with papers.

3. As time goes by narrow the coverage of the papers to the areas the pup routinely chooses to eliminate.

4. When you are with your pup continue to abide by the three pillars: confine, supervise, and regulate. Make sure to get him to his papers when he needs to go until he starts doing so on his own.

5. Gradually start moving the papers towards the door and then get them outside. Once your pup starts looking for his papers outside you can begin to fade them out.

6. Use a dog walker, once your pup has had all his shots, to break up his day and give him an opportunity to eliminate outside.

7. Use a doggie door by pushing your pup's crate, minus the door, up to it and having an ex-pen on the other side. This will essentially force him to eliminate outside.

8. Keep your housebreaking benchmarks in mind. Your pup can't be considered reliably housebroken until:

    i.   He's six to eight months of age and

    ii. Hasn't had any accidents in the house for two months.

In the preceding pages I've talked at length about various approaches to housebreaking. An intelligent and diligent combination of these methods should lead you to accident-free puppy ownership in relatively short order. All that having been said, let's take a look at some common questions and problems that can arise when housebreaking your pup.

Frequently Asked Questions

Q: Should I train my dog to let me know when he needs to go outside?

A: No! It won't take him long to learn to manipulate you. I'll give you a great example. Some time ago a very good friend to mine taught her standard poodle to ring a bell that she had hung on the doorknob when he needed to eliminate. Being a poodle it took him all of about thirty seconds to figure this out and for about a week everything was fine. The dog would ring the bell three to four times a day, be let out, relieve himself and then come back in. Very soon, however, he learned that every time he rang the bell someone would run over and let him out. "Not a bad deal," he must have thought because by the second week he was ringing that bell about fifteen times a day demanding to be let out. Of course, as soon as he got out all he wanted to do was play. He had

THE PROBLEM WITH PAPER TRAINING

Paper training is something I only recommend when no other option is available simply because it teaches your pup to eliminate in the house. Avoid paper training unless absolutely necessary, for instance, if you're gone long periods of time or live in a high rise. If at all possible, teach your pup from day one to eliminate outside.

learned to train his owners to take him out on command.

Don't let your dog do that to you. It's your job to observe your dog, learn his habits and establish a pattern that both works with his habits and your routine. As he gets older he'll learn to expect to be taken out at certain times and you'll know through experience when he generally needs to go. Keep it like that and everyone will be happy.

Q: My pup is now eight months old but he still gets me up at 5:00 a.m. to go out because that was the habit we developed when he was young. It's not such a big problem during the week but it's annoying on the weekend when I'd like to sleep in. What should I do?

A: Once you've trained your puppy to sleep through the night you should not have to get up at any time other than when you feel like it. As he gets older teach him to wait to be let out until you're ready by reprimanding him for complaining. Use the squirt bottle or any of the other measures described in the first half of this section if needed. If you're no longer using a crate and are concerned that your dog will find some place in the house to eliminate simply tie him to the side of your bed or some other place during the night. This will have the same effect crating would, that is, keeping him in a small area. Since dogs do not like eliminating in the area where they sleep he'll work to contain himself until you're ready to take him out.

Q: Often, when I bring my dog outside he just stands there and looks at me or goes on a sniffing expedition although I know he has to defecate. Sometimes I stand out there for fifteen minutes waiting for him to do his business. I can't bring him back inside and then take him out fifteen minutes later because I need to leave. Is there anything I can do to speed this process up?

Don't be fooled. The coy thing is just an act.

A: Actually, yes. I used to have a German Shepherd pup that would do the same thing. But alas, I do have a bag of tricks and this situation called for a particularly dirty one. I simply took a paper match, held the sulphur end (the end that lights) between my fingers and inserted the paper end in the pup's rectum just like a thermometer (*be sure never to insert the sulphur end*). Then I'd just leave it there. That's right! Now this might seem a tad crude but what it does is start a reflex action in the dog that will generally have him defecating within five to ten seconds. If you prefer to be more clinical about it, glycerin suppositories will do the trick also. Once your pup starts eliminating be sure to repeat "hurry up" while he's doing it and reward with a treat when finished. Soon you won't need the gimmicks anymore. And rest assured, the peculiar feelings and possible hesitation you may experience the first time you try this will be quickly overcome by a feeling of satisfied accomplishment when your pup does his business in record time. Few things bring more joy to the owner of a new puppy than the sight of that puppy eliminating outside and on schedule. In a pinch (no pun intended) this little trick can help get you there.

If failure to urinate is your problem, simply overload his bladder before going out by offering your pup a large bowl of water with a little wet dog food mixed into it. If he's fully loaded and then starts an active walk, well, there's only so much he can hold.

Q: My young pup does not seem to understand that he shouldn't eliminate in his crate. Every time I look in there he's either urinated or defecated. What should I do?

A: Some dogs, for various reasons, usually revolving around unsanitary conditions in their surroundings at a very early age, do not have such a strong nesting instinct. This is

especially true of pet shop pups that are forced to eliminate in the cage behind the display window. By the time you get the pup home his nesting instinct has been essentially destroyed. To resolve this there are several things you can try. Often if the pup has too much room in the crate he will use one area to eliminate in and another to sleep in. Reducing the size of the crate by putting a cardboard box or some other obstruction in it often solves this problem. Similarly, some pups will pee on their bedding which conveniently absorbs the spill and gets it out of the way. Therefore, removing the bedding is often helpful as well. You should also ask yourself if you're taking your pup out frequently enough. Perhaps he can't hold it as long as you'd like just yet.

If you've done all these things and continue to have problems, try either using a tie down instead of a crate or creating a confinement area using an ex-pen. Then put your pup's crate in the area with the door open and cover the entire area in papers. Given a choice your pup will eliminate outside his crate on the papers and break the habit of soiling in the crate, potentially rebuilding his nesting instinct. After a few weeks begin crating your pup again, though for very short periods (no more than an hour or two) and take him outside as frequently as possible.

If despite your best efforts you continue to have problems perhaps you should check with your vet to see if there's some physiological problem.

Q: Every time I go to pet my dog he pees right in front of me. He's shameless. What should I do?

A: There are two types or urination that are not a function of housebreaking, *excitement* and *submissive urination*.

Some pups, when the owners come home or when anyone approaches them, become so excited that they literally cannot contain themselves. The moment you look at them they immediately squat and pee – shamelessly. This is called excitement urination. Other pups, being of an extremely deferential disposition, express their submissive attitude by rolling over on their back and peeing. This is the single most submissive thing a pup can do and what he's telling you is that he totally defers to your authority. These types of urination can co-exist in the same pup and more commonly occur in females, though males can display them as well. Most pups usually grow out of this by the end of the first year though with a few, like my own, a trace of the behavior can linger for years. What they have in common is that *reprimanding your pup for displaying such behaviors is guaranteed to make them worse!*

The fact is that such elimination is an involuntary physical by-product of an emotional condition. Thus the only way to effectively deal with it is to deal with the emotional condition. If your pup is very excitable you must avoid exciting him at greeting times and if your pup is very submissive you must avoid making him feel the need to express his submission.

The solution to both problems is essentially the same: *Never enthusiastically greet a pup like this.* Do exactly the opposite, downplay your greetings or even ignore him. By ignore I mean *don't look at him, speak to him or touch him* on your initial encounter. Instead, turn your side to him, look away from him and for all practical purposes pretend you don't have a pup. It's only when he begins to settle down (in the case of excitable urination) or become less submissive (in the case of submissive urination) that you should begin to engage the dog. And even when you do the engagement should be very low-key with you maintaining a tone and attitude that does not cause your pup to become too excited or take too deferential an attitude towards you. Turning your body sideways, kneeling, avoiding eye contact, maintaining silence and letting your pup come to you are very helpful. As your pup's energy, excitement, and/or submission level decreases you can proportionately increase your level of engagement.

If you at any point reprimand your pup for this behavior (which is, as stated above, completely involuntary) he will believe that he has to act more submissively or he will become more excited in either case exacerbating your problem. If you then respond by getting even angrier you set up a vicious cycle. Patience, understanding and a cool head are what's required to get past this issue.

Q: I find that my pup is basically housetrained but that there are a couple of spots in the house that he still habitually eliminates in.

A: Begin by cleaning the area with an enzymatic solution specifically designed to eliminate dog odors from an area, such as *Nature's Miracle* or Doctor's Foster and Smith's *Dogtergent*. Once the area is clean begin feeding your pup his meals there. Dogs do not like to eliminate in areas where they eat. This should stop him from returning to eliminate there relatively quickly. However, be sure to keep a good eye on him for a while in order to keep him from moving his toilet to some other area in the house. Remember, effective supervision is essential to successful housebreaking.

If the spot the puppy is hitting is in a part of the house that is not frequented too often spend a little more time playing with him there and teach him that it is part of his space. Some pups will view rooms they don't spend much time in as areas outside their living space thus making them fair game for a nice spot to relieve themselves. Making those areas a part of what the dog views as his den will tend to resolve the problem.

Q: I'd like to take my puppy out on a regular routine basis but I don't have a yard and my vet told me not to let him outside on the street until he's had all of his vaccinations. What do I do?

A: This was precisely the position I found myself in with my most recent pup. My housetraining plan ran headlong into the veterinary injunction not to let my pup out. So I arranged a compromise. Since the vet's concern was that my pup not be exposed to the parvovirus outside I chose to wash down an area of the sidewalk outside my home with a mixture of one part bleach and seven parts water twice to three times a day. This mixture will basically kill anything infectious on contact and made the area safe for my pup. While this was tedious and time consuming it did help achieve the desired end which was to eliminate accidents in the house in relatively short order.

Q: My pup got sick from something he picked up outside and had terrible diarrhea. Although he seemed practically housetrained he's since completely reverted.

A: When your pup is sick, all bets are off. Your pup can't help himself so it's your job to keep an eye on him and get him out more often. If, once the pup's health improves, he has indeed reverted in his housetraining habits you should go back to square one: confine, supervise and regulate. His reversion will be overcome relatively quickly once he gets reacquainted with his old habits.

Q: My pup eats feces!

This, to a human, is pehaps the single most disgusting thing a pup can do. Yet strangely, from many pup's point of view nothing could be better. If your pup is eating his own poop the good news is, it's harmless. The bad news is that it's just so gross. There are several products on the market such as Forbid and Deter that you can add to your pup's diet that can help. You can also use a strong "off" command (see p.152) to teach him that this is a major no-no or spike the pile with Bitter Apple Spray,

Courtesy: Deirdre Lieberson

Lilly, a petite, polite pug at seven weeks.

Tabasco sauce, Cayenne pepper or Chinese hot chili oil. Be sure not to let your pup see you setting the trap. Sometimes, however, the best option is a quick and simple clean-up.

In the preceding pages I have covered 98% of all conceivable housetraining situations. Diligent application of these principles will lead you to a housetrained puppy relatively quickly. Remember, and I am repeating this only for emphasis, that you cannot consider your pup reliably housebroken until he's six to eight months of age and he's had no accidents in the house for two months. That doesn't mean you shouldn't stop having accidents way before then – you should if you're diligent about confining, supervising and regulating – it just means that given the opportunity your pup may still eliminate in the house.

Having covered housebreaking, it's time to move to the next group of topics, setting the tone for your pup's overall orientation to you, his immediate environment and life as a whole.

Setting the Tone I
Building the Right Relationship

Introduction

As I mentioned at the outset of this book, during the first four months or so of your pup's life he's in what is referred to as his critical socialization period. It is during this time that his primary orientation towards life as a whole is set. That includes his relationship with you. It is during this formative period that you should help your pup learn the rules of the human world as distinct from those of the dog world.

While those two worlds do actually have a great deal in common there are also some significant differences. Let's take a quick look at both and see how we can build a bridge between them. Dogs are pack animals. So are people. Both species are intensely social and as such have developed various forms of communication, mostly unspoken, which gives clues as to the nature of their relationship and thus grease the wheels of social interaction.

In many cases canine body language is even similar to human body language. For example, with dogs direct sustained eye contact is often viewed as a challenge. The same is true with people. To a dog a hand on a shoulder as a form of greeting can be viewed pushy and inappropriate while a scratch on the chest or under the chin is readily accepted. Similarly with

A Change in Scenery

When you first bring your pup home the only social experience he's generally had has been with his mom and his littermates. While mom has served primarily as a milk bar, a fuzzy home base and occasional enforcer of limited behavior boundaries, his littermates have been his primary source of entertainment and interaction. When you bring your pup into your home it is immediately clear to him that you're not mom and it's therefore natural for him to lump you into the category of littermate. Now, with his littermates your pup's experience has been that life is simply a free for all. He can chase them, tackle them, bite them and generally be as rough and tumble as he wants. One of the primary purposes of the exercises in this chapter is to teach him that you're not a littermate. Once you've convinced him of this his inclination to bite you will diminish dramatically. If, simultaneously, he is getting plenty of opportunities to socialize with other puppies (see p.128) he will find an appropriate outlet for his need to bite and accordingly feel even less of a need to exercise his jaws on you.

people, we don't greet each other with a slap on the back on our first encounter. We shake hands. The list goes on. The point is that from a social standpoint dogs and humans have a lot in common and one of the things that makes dogs such wonderful pets is that they readily transfer all their pack instincts to their human companions.

However, the one area where dogs and humans most commonly tend to part company is around the issue of hierarchy. As I've already mentioned at the outset of this book (see p.26) dogs crave structure and leadership and without it both their mental health and their ability to assimilate themselves into a human world are seriously compromised. This is a point that a great many dog owners fail to grasp and such failure leads to innumerable serious problems

OUT OF AFRICA

Recently I was watching a special on the Discovery Channel about elephants that I found very instructive in relation to dog behavior. The documentary was about a group of baby elephants that had been orphaned when their parents were murdered by poachers. The rangers decided to transport all of the calves to a protected national park where they would be released and allowed to grow up together. At least they'd have each other, the reasoning went. Several years passed uneventfully and it seemed that all was going well. However, at some point things got ugly. For no apparent reason the now adolescent male elephants seemed to be going on rampages, killing rhinos (also endangered), threatening local villagers, tearing up large areas of forest, and generally growing increasingly dangerous. Park rangers were baffled by this uncharacteristically violent behavior and feared that they might have to destroy these elephants whom they'd worked so hard to save. Before resorting to such a radical solution a number of behaviorists were brought in, most of whom seemed equally baffled.

As I was sitting there watching it became exceedingly clear to me, based on my experience with dogs, what was going on and I was shocked that the behaviorists had not identified the problem. Eventually one of them hit on it. These adolescent males, pumped up by hormones and filled with their own power, were running rampant because, as far as they could see, they were the ultimate authority in their environment. There was no one around to put limits on their behavior with power and authority. The solution was to fly in a couple of huge, domineering, adult males and mix them into this group. This worked like a charm. In a couple of shots they showed these enormous elephants backing down the adolescent punks who were visibly shocked by the commanding presence of their elders. The violent disruptions these youngsters had caused ceased immediately. Of course, the point is that authority and well-defined behavior boundaries are indispensable in raising a well-adjusted individual of any species, including your dog.

between dogs and their people. A dog must know his place in his human pack and he will be perfectly happy even if his place is at the bottom (where it should be) so long as he is consistently made aware that this is his place. It is uncertainty about their place in the pack that drives so many puppies to act out in ways that are totally inappropriate and ultimately even dangerous (they don't remain puppies forever, after all). It causes them to keep pushing and pushing until they find the outer limits of the behavior boundaries. If they never find any they just get crazier and crazier. Therefore your job as the owner of a new pup is to help him to understand his place in the pack using methods that appeal and make sense to his canine nature. To this end I will outline a number of exercises that will teach your pup very quickly about your leadership role and which will expose any potential behavior problems early on.

These exercises are designed to teach your pup two things. First, they will teach him to trust you. That is, your pup will learn to *trust* that no matter what you're doing, even if it's slightly uncomfortable or annoying, you're not going to harm him and that you always have his best interests at heart. Second, your pup will learn to *respect* you. In other words, he'll learn that no matter what you're doing to him, he has no right to complain, struggle, whine and most importantly, bite. The fact is, throughout your pup's life there will be all kinds of people, yourself included, that will have to handle him in ways he might find annoying. That would include veterinarians, groomers, walkers, kennel owners and a host of other dog professionals. Dogs who bite or threaten these caregivers quickly find themselves isolated and needing heavy sedation to have even the most routine procedures performed on them. On the other hand, teaching your puppy to accept such handling in stride opens the doors to a multitude of experiences without which the quality of his life would be seriously compromised.

THE ZERO TOLERANCE BITE POLICY

In my approach to puppy raising I teach the pup that it is never okay to put his teeth on a person for any reason at any time. This is in direct contradiction to many trainers who believe that it's okay for the pup to put his teeth on you so long as he does it gently. Such an approach doesn't make any sense to me. I can't think of one good reason why a dog should be allowed to put his mouth on a person, even gently. All this does is create a gray area out of what should really be a black and white issue – you never bite anyone, period. Try explaining to the mother of a five year old, who was startled and pulled away from the "gentle mouthing" of your dog only to end up with a cut, that your dog didn't really bite him. Or try convincing the person who just had his fingers crushed when your dog tried to take a tennis ball out of his hands that "he was just playing." Throughout this book you will find exercises designed to deeply imprint your pup with the idea that he's simply never to put his mouth on people, whether intentional or not, for any reason whatsoever. Please don't underestimate the importance of this point.

In short, trust and respect are the foundation of any successful relationship including the one with your pup and the exercises outlined below will help you to teach him both. Before embarking take a moment to consider the temperament of your pup. If you have a shy pup (p.14) you might go a little easy with these exercises in the beginning while if you have a pushy pup (p.16) you might have to hang on for dear life right from the start.

LEARNING TO A LITTLE HANDLE PRESSURE

Aside from teaching your pup to trust and respect you, the handling exercises described in this section also teach your pup to tolerate a little physical and emotional pressure. It would be hard to overestimate the importance of this. I have met too many older dogs who'd never had any demands placed on them early in life and that when faced with any kind of pressure in training or in life just crumbled emotionally. They simply couldn't handle it. Training such a dog is exceedingly difficult and trying for both dog and owner.

A dog, like a person, must learn to handle pressure in increasing increments as they get older. This builds a certain emotional and physical resilience to the vicissitudes of life. Consider the case of people. When kids are young the pressures of their lives are nominal – a few behavior boundaries around the house and small assignments from their first grade class. However, as they get older the demands on them increase gradually and by the time they're in their early twenties they can handle the extraordinary pressure of notoriously challenging things like medical school and law school. Had they not been exposed to increasing degrees of pressure throughout their developmental years they simply wouldn't be able to hack the demands of such intense situations, they would just emotionally collapse.

The same is true for your pup so please be diligent in practicing these exercises. And finally, also bear in mind that the person who puts the most pressure on a dog in a fair way gets the lion's share of the dog's love, affection and respect.

Exercise #1 Cradling your puppy

Scoop your puppy up into your arms and hold him belly up as if you were cradling a baby. One arm should support his back while the hand of the other arm is gently placed over the puppy's chest in order to hold him in place. For a puppy this position is very vulnerable and submissive and most will struggle to some degree in order to escape from it. If your pup struggles keep him firmly in place with the hand that is on his chest and issue the command "settle" in a firm tone. The moment the pup calms down and ceases struggling gently massage him with the hand holding his chest and praise him with soft tones. This will begin to teach him that the end of the struggle equates with the beginning of pleasure. If he continues to remain calm and settled you can reward him with a little treat (keep a small pile nearby just for the occasion). In the beginning, most puppies will alternate between struggling and relaxing so you have to be able to be a bit like Jekyll and Hyde, alternating in rapid succession between being firm and sweet. How much your pup struggles will depend largely on whether he's more of a shy or pushy type.

Whichever he is, it is extremely important during this exercise to *never release the puppy while he is struggling.* This will only teach him that physically struggling against you is an acceptable strategy for

Scoop him into your lap and...

Restrain him if he struggles...

If he bites...

Grab his muzzle and reprimand...

When he settles, reward him with a treat.

getting out of doing what you want him to do and can easily bleed over into other areas of his relationship with you. Holding on at all costs can occasionally prove challenging as some puppies may throw an outright temper tantrum or scream as if you're torturing them. However, no matter what happens you must continue with the exercise until your puppy relaxes.

Now, in the course of this temper tantrum many puppies will attempt to bite and nip. No matter the degree of intensity, whether mild or maniacal, this is the time to teach your pup that *he is never to bite you.* There are two ways to respond. First, the moment you feel your puppy's teeth on your skin, with lighting speed grab his muzzle firmly and in a reprimanding tone command "no biting" in his face. Continue to hold the pup's muzzle closed until he begins to relax, making sure that he can breathe and that you're not clamping his teeth down on his tongue. Remember, *the idea is not to be mean but meaningful.* Grabbing a dog's muzzle and holding it closed is a very effective form of reprimand since it is something the pup is already familiar with. This is one way that dogs reprimand each other. Keep in mind that when a dog reprimands another dog that reprimand is intensely explosive, perfectly timed, physically harmless and over as fast as it started. If you can reprimand your pup in this manner it won't take him long to get the message. After all, you're speaking canine, a language he understands. Once the reprimand is over and the pup has settled down, immediately resume stroking him gently.

If you find that you're simply physically incapable of executing this maneuver there is a second option. Have handy a bottle of Bitter Apple spray, a taste

THOSE NASTY LITTLE TEETH

Ever wonder why pups have those razor sharp teeth? Well, part of the reason obviously is because large adult teeth wouldn't fit into such a tiny mouth. But there are also important behavioral reasons for those little teeth and why they are so painful. First, they help mom to know when it's time to start weaning her pups. Those knife-like teeth digging into her nipples are a major disincentive to continue allowing the pups to nurse. Additionally, and perhaps most importantly, they teach the puppy about bite inhibition. For example, if two pups are playing together and one pup bites really hard the other pup will respond in one of two ways. It will either yelp and run away or it will turn around and really nail the offending pup with a bite of its own. In the first case the biter loses a playmate, in the second case he gets reprimanded. Either result is undesirable and begins to teach the pup to ease up on his biting. Bite inhibition must be learned by your pup during his critical socializing period or he will never be able to learn it. I'll have more to say about this in my discussion of puppy playgroups (p.130).

deterrent readily available at most pet stores, or Binaca, the breath spray, and quickly squirt it either directly into your pup's mouth or just in front of it at the moment he starts to bite and again bark "no biting." If you have a squirmy puppy this can be a two person job so get some help if needed. One person holds the pup while the other one sprays. Most puppies detest Binaca and especially Bitter Apple, often spitting and foaming at the mouth in disgust, yet it is totally harmless and amazingly effective. Soon your puppy will learn that biting is a seriously counter-productive behavior. When he begins to relax go back to your soothing tone of voice, gentle massage and occasional treats, being sure to release him only when he is no longer struggling.

You should practice this exercise with your puppy as often as possible throughout the day, *especially when he is totally worked up and not in the mood.* This will begin to teach him that you have the right to handle him in any way you see fit no matter what he's doing at the moment and that "resistance is futile." Your overall goal should be to have your puppy so relaxed in your arms that he could easily fall asleep there. Continue to do this exercise, as well as those that follow, throughout not only early puppyhood but through adolescence and well into adulthood. This will keep him conditioned to accept your handling even as he grows older and physically more confident. If your pup gets too big to cradle in your arms, simply cradle him between your outstretched legs.

Exercise #2 Hold your puppy flat on his side

This exercise is essentially an extension of the previous one. Place the puppy on the floor on his side and restrain him there by putting one hand on his hip and the other on his shoulder. The same rules outlined above apply here as well, i.e., *no struggling and no biting* and the same reprimands apply as well. If you're using a taste deterrent be sure to keep it handy. After all, timing is of the essence. Once the puppy relaxes grab his legs and gently roll him onto his other side, repeating the procedure. Your goal is to be able to roll your pup easily from side to side while his attitude remains completely relaxed.

Hold your puppy on his side...

Then flip him over...

And hold him on the other side. Praise and reward calm behavior.

Exercise # 3 The Body Exam

This exercise should be practiced in conjunction with both of the previous ones. With your pup either cradled or on his side begin giving him a gentle examination of his entire body making sure to cover all the sensitive areas. Touch his feet, gently push his toenails out as you might for clipping, rub the insides of his legs, stretch them back and forth, touch his tail, his ears and even lift his lips, look at his teeth and massage his gums. Again, there should be no biting or struggling. When doing the side to side exercise be sure to examine both sides of his body. Once again continue to do these exercises throughout not only the critical socializing period but through at least the first year of your puppy's life.

Gently stretch his legs back and forth through a full range of motion...

Open his mouth and massage his gums...

Put your fingers between his toes...

Now that's a happy puppy!

Exercise #4 Stand, Sit, Down

In this exercise you will physically move your puppy through three positions that he will learn as commands later: stand, sit and down. *You will issue no commands at this point as this is a handling exercise not a training exercise.* It builds on what you've done up to this point and continues to condition the puppy to being handled in a variety of ways. Later in your pup's development, when you have to correct him for failure to comply with a command that he clearly knows, you will be able to use these handling exercises as a form of correction. For example, if, once your dog knows the command sit, he suddenly refuses to comply – which he inevitably will at some point – you will be able to quickly handle him into the position using the sit component of this handling exercise.

Begin by placing one hand under your pup's chin, the other under his abdomen and holding him in a standing position. Keep him in this position until he stops squirming using the "settle" command if you have to. Then keeping one hand under his chin remove the other

Then scoop his hips...

With one hand under his belly and one under his chin, hold him in a stand...

...into a sit (do not push his hips)...

hand from under his abdomen, place it at the top of his shoulder and run it across his back, down and around his rump, gently scooping his hind legs into a sit position. *Never push down on the pup's hips.* This can put unnecessary pressure on his hips. Make sure to *gently scoop his rear end under.* No force should be necessary in this exercise. Simple leverage should be sufficient to do the trick.

Once your pup is comfortably seated slide his front legs out and scoop him into a down position. Again, try and use leverage here. With your puppy in front of you, place one hand on the front leg closest to you and the other onto his shoulder. Then gently pull the leg closest to you out while using your other hand to bring his shoulder in the direction of the leg just pulled out thus sliding him into a down position. Again, no force should be required here. Just simple maneuvering of his body.

Once your pup is in the down position you can repeat the cycle by scooping him back up into the stand position. As with the other exercises, if your puppy responds to any of this with an attempt to bite you, or even gently mouth you, a very firm reprimand is in order.

leverage his shoulder down in the direction of that leg...

Then pull out his front leg and...

Then repeat the procedure...

This first set of four exercises – cradling, laying on the side, the body exam and the stand/sit/down routine – form the foundation on which you will add more exercises in due course (refer to the timeline on page 211 for the appropriate order in which to introduce these exercises). Before adding new exercises, however, please be sure you are having no trouble with any of the above, *especially with biting.* Keep in mind that the primary purpose of these drills is to teach your pup to accept all kinds of handling without biting. Most puppies will adapt to this routine within a matter of days and even very difficult puppies should have absorbed it all within a couple of weeks. But no matter how long it takes please stay with it and remember, practice makes perfect. As rock legend Mick Jagger is reported to have once said "too much is never enough."

Once you have all this well in hand it's time to add a few new routines.

Exercise 5 "Say Aaaah!"

In this exercise you will teach your pup to allow you to open his mouth and take a look around in there. Ironically, you're setting up a double standard. That is, you want your pup to understand that he's to never put his teeth on human skin for any reason, period, yet at the same time he should allow you to put your hand in his mouth anytime you like. While seemingly contradictory this is actually a relatively simple thing to teach.

Begin with your pup in a relaxed position such as a sit, cradle or lying on his side. Then gently bring one hand over his muzzle and place your fingers under his lips just behind the canine teeth. This should give you enough leverage to carefully pry his mouth open. *Be careful not to pinch his lips against his teeth.* When your pup's mouth is open even a little bit you can use your other hand to help open it a bit further by slowly opening his lower jaw. By the time you attempt this exercise your pup should know better than to bite in response to handling, however, if he does you know what to do. As long as your pup is not struggling excessively (a little bit is normal in the beginning) tell him what a good boy he is and quickly drop a treat in his mouth. Even if you've only managed to get him to open his mouth a half inch for half a second go ahead and drop a treat in it. You want to convince him that having his mouth opened by you is a good thing. Steadily continue working with this exercise until your pup will allow his mouth to be held open for at least ten seconds *without a struggle*.

Conditioning your pup like this early will allow you to brush his teeth, pull things out, and examine his mouth for any reason with ease.

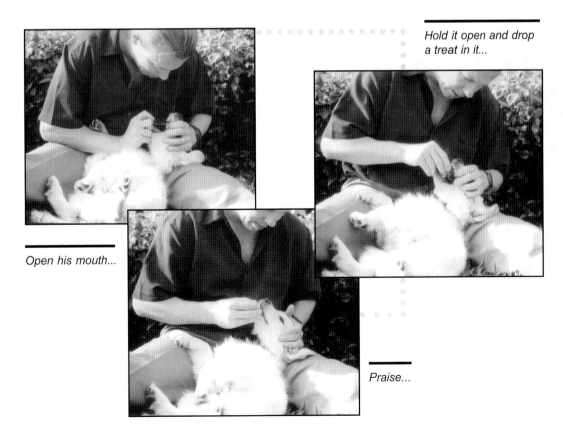

Hold it open and drop a treat in it...

Open his mouth...

Praise...

Exercise #6 Muzzle grab and forehead kiss

Many adult dogs take great offense at direct face-to-face contact with people. From a canine standpoint this is interpreted as a challenge. Getting in a dog's face is one of the most common scenarios leading to bites. However, since people seem to have a great predilection for this sort of greeting it makes sense to teach your pup early on that such overtures from humans are not necessarily meant to challenge. Therefore the pup can learn to take it in stride and even appreciate it for the form of affection that it is.

Grab his muzzle gently...

That's the purpose of this very simple handling exercise. Approach your puppy from the front, gently grab his muzzle and hold it at a slightly downward angle, one that will allow you to plant a kiss square on his forehead. Be sure to do this exercise in the context of great affection so your pup learns that the two go together. If you've done the exercises outlined above you should really have no trouble with this one at all and, as with all of these exercises, more is better, so practice, practice, practice.

and plant a big, fat kiss on his forehead...

Don't forget to refer to the Puppy Primer Timeline on page 211 for the proper order in which to introduce all the exercises in this book!

Exercise #7 Rough Him Up

Take your puppy and handle him a bit roughly. Pinch his ear, pull his tail, lay him down on his side and spin him around, do anything you can to annoy him *short of actually hurting him*. After each action give him a treat and be sure to do this in a context that is playful. If he attempts to express his annoyance by mouthing or biting, firmly reprimand him with a muzzle grab or a squirt of your taste deterrent while issuing the phrase "no biting" sharply. Be sure only to attempt this exercise once the other ones are well in hand, so to speak

Why in the world would I suggest roughing up your pup? Think about it for a minute. Under what circumstances is a dog most likely to get handled in this manner? When children are involved, of course. If a dog has never been handled like this and is always treated as if he were made of porcelain when the day comes that a child, or anyone for that matter, starts climbing all over him in annoying ways he may feel he is being attacked and respond accordingly. Teach your pup to handle rough, even slightly inappropriate, handling. Help him to understand that people sometimes do things inadvertently that might annoy him and that this is no reason to bite them. Doing so could spare you the distinct unpleasantness of a lawsuit.

CASE HISTORY

I recently received a call from a very nice couple whose dog had just bitten someone in the calf rather severely, resulting in a trip to the hospital and multiple stitches. According to them this was an ordinarily very nice dog who had never shown an iota of aggression towards anyone. What had happened was that they were having a party and the dog was curled up in a corner when someone accidentally stepped on her toe. The dog immediately leaped up and severely bit the person on the leg. "Well, that's understandable" you might say to yourself and it might well be. However, it was also totally avoidable. Further investigation revealed that these very well intentioned owners had been extremely careful from day one not to "mishandle" the dog, never to treat it roughly or harshly and, in short, always to walk on eggshells around it. Because the dog had never experienced any kind of rough handling it had no choice but to draw the conclusion that the sudden pain it experienced from this person must be an attack and that she had to defend herself with whatever means she could. Had she been habituated to some roughhousing as a young pup in all likelihood this bite would not have happened.

Puppies, Children and Handling Exercises

If you have children in the house it's important that they learn these handling exercises as well. However, since children are smaller and less coordinated than adults you should habituate your pup to the exercises first and only when you're no longer having trouble with biting should you introduce them to your kids. Of course, when the kids are doing the exercises you should be diligently supervising them and, if necessary, reprimand your pup. If your children are very young you can place them in your lap, take their hands and move them through the exercises and if you have an infant you can do the same thing with the little one in one of those Baby Bjorn™ child carriers. For more information about dogs and children please read my book *There's a Baby in the House: Preparing your Dog for the Arrival of your Child.*

The above mentioned handling exercises, while simple, are among the most important things you can teach your puppy during his critical socializing period. They imprint your dominance on him at an early age – an imprint he will carry with him throughout his life – and help to put out of his mind permanently the idea that biting people in the course of the ordinary circumstances of his life is ever okay. In short, they are your best insurance policy against the inappropriate biting of humans. And the truth is that while you can live with a dog that doesn't sit too well and whose recall is a little sloppy, it's very difficult to live with a dog that bites. So if you get nothing from this book other than a dog that doesn't bite it will have been worth the price of admission. For this reason, while these exercises should be introduced as early as possible they should be vigorously pursued at the very least through your pup's first year.

DOMINANCE IMPRINTING

Several years ago I had a wonderful client who was heavily involved with horses. In fact, she had actually purchased a foal before it was born and had arranged with her trainer to be present the day of the foal's birth. Now, the interesting thing about horses is that being flight animals (as opposed to dogs which are prey animals) they are born relatively intact and ready to run within a relatively short period of time after their birth. In fact, shortly after their birth they will attempt to stand. When this point came my client's trainer instructed her to gently embrace and restrain the foal in order to prevent it from getting up. She repeated this procedure several times before finally actually helping the foal to stand. The point of all this, the trainer informed her, was to imprint her physical dominance on this foal the moment it entered the world. This would be an impression that would last a lifetime and aid all future training in a dramatic way.

Dominance imprinting works in people also. Who hasn't seen (or been) an otherwise assertive and confident full-grown man or woman become like a meek little sheep in front of their elderly parents? While we clearly don't have to submit to the older and weaker we do because their relationship of dominance was imprinted so strongly on us so consistently for such a long period of time that it stays with us for a lifetime. It's the same thing with our pups. The more we imprint our dominance on them from the earliest times the less likely we'll be to have trouble with them as they get older.

SETTING THE TONE II OR TEACHING YOUR PUP WHAT YOU DON'T WANT HIM TO DO

INTRODUCTION

I've mentioned several times that anything your pup gets used to during the first four or so months of his life he'll probably never have a problem dealing with and anything that he doesn't get used to during that time frame he'll have an increasingly difficult time adapting to. I've gone over housebreaking and some exercises you can do to set the tone for your pup's relationship with you but you must also acclimate your pup to his new environment, a human world where many of his natural instincts will tend to get him into trouble. In short, you must *socialize* him.

When I use the term socialization I'm using it in a very broad sense: *an acclimation to his total environment which includes his relationship to people, objects, experiences and other dogs.* Proper socialization prevents not only undesirable behaviors in the home but also phobic behaviors that can lead to all sorts of problems as your pup gets older, including aggression. A fundamental rule that you might keep in mind throughout the very early stages of your pup's life is this: *anything that you want him to be able to deal with as an adult get him used to it **now** and anything that you don't want him to do as an adult, prevent it **now**.* Dogs are creatures of habit and as the old saying goes, "an ounce of prevention is worth a pound of cure."

Let's begin with things you don't want your pup to do as an adult dog.

Jumping up

Every puppy seems to have an irrepressible urge to jump up on anyone that comes near him. This is understandable. One way a lower ranking dog greets a higher ranking dog is by licking its muzzle, an act both of submission and affection. The problem, of course, is that the pup is oh, so small and you, by comparison, are so very large that the only way he feels he can bridge the gap between himself and your face is by jumping up on you. Now, many owners think it's very cute when their eight-week old Rottweiler is trying to climb up their leg in an uninhibited show of affection and reward the attempt by lifting the pup up and showering him with affection. Many of their friends think it's cute too…for a while. Soon, however, neither owner nor friends are going to be so amused when a now eight month old, ninety-five pound Rottweiler is doing the same thing. Trying to break a habit that's been reinforced since early puppyhood is much more difficult than never allowing the habit to develop in the first place. As hard as it might be, given your pup's cuteness, discourage him from jumping up from day one. There are numerous ways to do this so I'll just review a few.

Whoa boy!

The first one involves simply shoving your pup off you with your hands on his chest the moment he even begins to come up on you while gruffly saying "ah, ah, ah," or "off." Then quickly use your

---

FACE TIME

Ever wonder why dogs like to lick faces? Most of us like to believe that it's a canine kiss, an expression of our dog's affection toward us, and to some degree that's true. But the origin of the behavior goes back to the young pup licking at the muzzle of the mother dog which in turn would cause her to regurgitate food for him. In the course of licking mom's muzzle the pup is also learning to take on a submissive and ingratiating attitude which all gets mixed together with motherly love and physical nourishment. So when your pup licks your muzzle it is indeed a warm show of affection and not simply and effort to get you to spit something up as many clinical behaviorists would have you believe.

hands, which are already on the pup, to scoop him into a sit using the handling exercise from the previous section and immediately begin petting and praising him once in position. Have everyone in your household do the same thing and soon your pup will learn that the affection and attention he's looking for will automatically come to him the moment he sits and that jumping up will only get a gruff response. What you'll usually find, if you're consistent, is that after some time your pup will approach you and take a sit position as a form of greeting. Of course the first time he does that (and the second, third, fourth…) you should immediately reward him with a flood of affection. Too many pups get ignored when they're doing the right thing and thus precious opportunities to positively reinforce desirable behaviors are lost. *Remember, catch him doing something right!*

While this method might be effective for you and members of your family it's unlikely that your friends are going to be able to pull this off without some instruction. At those times when your pup is jumping up on hapless guests there are several other solutions you might employ. The first involves simply leashing the pup when you know guests are arriving and standing on the leash at the point where it touches the floor (this should be easy if you're using the umbilical cord approach to supervision described on p.49). This way, every time the pup jumps up he automatically gets a little correction. Very soon he'll begin to inhibit himself and then your job, of course, is to bend over and give him his longed for affection. Once again he learns that one behavior is counter-productive and the other gets him what he wants.

Another option involves a squirt bottle filled with water. Be sure the bottle is the kind that allows you to shoot a jet stream. Hook the trigger in your pants

PREPARE FOR THE WORST… AND THE BEST

As you've already seen, managing a small puppy is a lot of work. Whenever someone sends me a young pup for preliminary training I prepare myself thoroughly, knowing that at any moment I might have to reprimand, praise or restrain the pup. I hook a squirt bottle in one pocket in order to efficiently correct unwanted behaviors. I keep a baggie full of delicious treats in the other pocket so I can "catch the pup doing something right" and reinforce him for it immediately. And finally, I keep him tied to me on a leash or nearby on a tie down. At the very least he's dragging the leash around and I'm keeping an eye on him. In this way I've covered all my bases and can very quickly move the pup into behaviors I like and move him away from those I don't.

pocket and you'll have the bottle available like a six-shooter whenever you need it. Now, the moment your pup jumps up on you or someone else quickly squirt him in the nose while again commanding "off" in a firm tone (see p.152 for more information on this command). Try not to let your pup see the bottle thus learning that it's the bottle that's the problem and not your command. This is called *equipment orientation* and could teach him to respond only if he sees the bottle. In other words, squirting your pup should be like sniper fire. He should be unsure as to exactly where it came from and should suspect that you have this mysterious ability to spray him available at all times. If you are consistent with this your pup's impulse to jump up should diminish rather quickly. Once again, the moment he visibly inhibits himself quickly guide him into a sit and praise him wildly. For those pups that don't mind having water squirted on them try the Bitter Apple spray mentioned earlier. That should get his attention. You'll be amazed how quickly your pup will learn not to jump up if you use these methods consistently.

Courtesy: Mary Watson

Woody at ten weeks.

Now, I understand that some owners like their dogs to jump up on them and thus don't want to eliminate this behavior entirely. In fact, I myself am one of those owners. The way I handled these seemingly conflicting desires was to solidly teach my pup that she's never to jump up on me no matter what. This was the baseline behavior, the default position, that I enforced with her until she was about eight months old. Once this was totally clear I taught her that it's okay to jump up on me, and me only, when she hears the command "c'mon up" accompanied by a hand pat on my chest. She quickly picked this up and now I can have my cake and eat it too. But to get to this point I had to be patient and persistent in establishing the baseline position as one of never jumping up, period. If you're that consistent you'll get the same results.

Nipping and biting at our clothes, shoes and other extensions of our bodies

Related to jumping up is nipping and tearing at your clothes, shoes and the occasional loose finger. Several times a day your puppy will go through short but intense bursts of activity. Behavioral scientists, with all their flair for the English language, refer to them as "frenetic random activity periods," (FRAPs), a rather dull but accurate description of these displays. I simply refer to them as the puppy "getting the wild hair." During these outbursts your pup will tear around the house in a frenzy, jump up and grab anything in sight, including the aforementioned items, and generally act like the Tasmanian Devil of Bugs Bunny fame. While not limited to them, it is often during these displays that your pup will grab and tear at you, a behavior that, while sometimes cute, is more often annoying and potentially dangerous. Remember our zero tolerance biting policy? Please enforce it here as well.

The simplest way to do this is by once again using your trusty squirt bottle. Simply wait for your pup to act out and then relentlessly go after him and reprimand him with "off" commands and squirts in the nose (see p.152 for more information on this command as well as p.211 for the appropriate order in which to introduce all these concepts). Keep in mind that your timing must be perfect. Absolutely never let him get away with this as it will only set the stage for potentially serious problems down the road.

This squirt bottle method of correcting jumping is also very useful if you have kids in the house that are in the habit of getting the pup worked up, thus causing him to jump and nip at them. Since kids are usually too young and uncoordinated to effectively

reprimand the pup it's your job to shadow him like a ninja with the squirt bottle and give him a splash on the nose the moment he begins. In my view, it should not be necessary to have your children stop playing the way they like to in order to avoid working the puppy up. Remember, you're trying to integrate your pup into your household and condition him to its realities, not re-structure your entire life around the pup's sensibilities. And frankly, it's easier to teach your pup not to nip than to prevent your kids from playing wildly. Of course, there might be times when the most sensible thing to do is simply put the puppy in his crate, give him a bone to chew on and let the kids have their free for all. But I would most definitely encourage you to teach your pup how to play with your kids at their wildest without nipping and biting. Seems sensible, doesn't it?

Excessive barking

All dogs bark and they do so for a variety of reasons. These include territoriality, playfulness, annoyance or simply getting attention. Barking is a natural behavior and expecting your pup never to bark is like asking a person never to speak. While with some folks this might be a good idea, unfortunately it's simply not feasible. However, enough is enough. It's a good idea to teach your puppy a "quiet" command. The easiest way to do this is with your trusty squirt bottle. When your puppy begins to bark you should determine when you've heard enough and then issue the command "quiet" in a firm tone. The next sound that comes our of his mouth should be met instantly with a jet of water or Bitter Apple spray. Again, use the sniper fire approach but *be sure to give the pup a moment between the time you issue the "quiet" command and the time you squirt him.* Otherwise he has no chance to comply and learn how to avoid getting sprayed which is, after all, the whole point. Once your pup understands how to avoid getting sprayed and suspects that you might have that bottle on you at all times you'll be able to dispense with the bottle altogether and simply rely on the command "quiet."

If your pup is barking in your absence thus creating a problem with your neighbors, roommates, or anyone else in the immediate environment I would recommend a citronella spray collar (manufactured by Premier Pet products and available from various sources on the web. Prices vary widely so be sure to shop a little.) These collars are one hundred percent harmless, pain free and thus totally humane and okay for a puppy. They simply spray the pup under the muzzle with a jet of citronella spray – a lovely citrus scented essential oil that dogs, who seem to prefer only foul smells, detest – the moment the pup barks. Very quickly he will learn that when he's wearing that collar barking is a no-no. Over time he will also learn that certain situations demand silence. For instance, with my own pup I had chronic barking problems from early on. Now, one of the peculiarities of my own life at the time was that I ran a meditation center out of my home and people came there five days a week to meditate in silence. My dog barking in the other room was not especially conducive to this silence so at about two and a half months of age I fitted Zoë with her very own citronella collar. Of course the barking stopped immediately. She only had to get sprayed about three times before she figured out that this was a bad idea. But more interestingly, over the course of the next few months she learned that being locked in the bedroom between seven o'clock and eight o'clock at night was a situation that always demanded silence. I've never had to use the collar on her in that situation since.

What is Situational Learning?

Situational learning simply means that your pup can learn to associate certain situations with certain types of behavior. This can work both for you and against you. For example, if every time your pup approaches a curb you ask him to sit, soon he will begin sitting at curbs on his own. The same thing applies to doorways. On the other hand, many dogs learn that they should obey commands during obedience class but that the same level of responsiveness is not required at home. Thus they'll deliver two different standards of behavior depending on the situation in which they find themselves. In the example of my barking puppy, she learned that being locked up in a room between seven and eight o'clock at night was a situation which demanded silence and thus I no longer had to use the citronella collar on her. Keep an eye out for opportunities to exploit situational learning with your pup where it will help you (for example, teaching your pup to always walk near you when on a crowded sidewalk) and prevent it where it won't (don't teach your pup that at his favorite park he's never required to perform obedience exercises and that you're irrelevant in those situations).

Proper table manners

Puppies are naturally drawn to the good stuff we're eating even if they've had their fill of dog food and treats. And truthfully,  can you blame them? However, a dog pestering you for food while you're eating can be annoying to even the most avid dog lover. Your pup needs to learn some table manners early on. Now, table manners don't necessarily mean that you can't feed your dog from the table. It simply means propriety.

I can't begin to tell you how often I go to a client's home when somewhere during the session they proudly proclaim that they never feed their dog from the table, seeking to get some kind of look of

RIGHTS AND PRIVILEGES

When you were growing up, how many times did you hear your parents lecture you on the difference between rights and privileges? Plenty, I'm sure. The funny thing is, they were right and the same thing applies to your pup. Many trainers will tell you that you should never feed your dog from the table, let them up on the furniture, allow them in bed with you, etc...I heartily disagree – if you can teach your pup the difference between rights and privileges. If your pup grows up believing that he has some inherent right to participate in these things with you, you're going to have a problem. A dog with an entitlement mentality is a bite waiting to happen. On the other hand, if you can teach your pup that everything that comes to him is a privilege he has only through your good graces, then it's a whole other story. He will never take things for granted, he will always look to you for permission and direction and you can spoil him 'til the cows come home without adverse behavioral consequences. And after all, what's the fun of having a dog if you can't spoil him at least a little? Throughout this book you're learning ways of teaching your dog the difference between rights and privileges. Take them seriously and you'll have tons of fun with your dog; don't and you'll be in for a world of trouble.

approval from me for their ability to be a strict disciplinarian. I usually give them a wry smile and tell them that every dog trainer I know, myself included, feeds their dog from the table. There's usually a moment of stunned silence followed by "doesn't that teach them to beg, be annoying or not interested in their own food?" The answer is no, they learn what we teach them so let's teach them some manners.

To me table manners begin with the "out" command. "Out" simply means leave the area, now! Teaching it is very simple. Once more, take your squirt bottle in hand and put it behind your back. As your pup approaches you at the dinner table firmly command "out" accompanied by a wave of your hand as if you were throwing a person out. If your pup continues to approach, take a quick, assertive step towards him and squirt him simultaneously. As soon as he begins to back off, gently praise him. If thereafter he approaches you once more, repeat the procedure. Soon your pup will understand that "out" means leave the area. I usually demand six feet of clearance from him. In other words, "out" means you must get at least six feet away from me.

Clearly the way you'd use this command at the dinner table is to simply issue it, followed by a squirt if necessary, the moment your puppy enters what I call your "critical eating zone." Again, I define the critical eating zone as about six feet around all parts of the dinner table. If the pup enters the zone I issue the command "out" the first time and follow with a squirt from my bottle if he doesn't immediately back out. Any further intrusions and I don't warn the pup with the "out" command again, I simply spray him. Very soon he will learn that the "default" position at dinner time is don't come near the table. (If you don't wish to got to all this trouble you can also use the tie-down approach described in the sidebar on page 101).

Once you've established that baseline – allow six to eight months of your pup being totally kept out of the eating zone – you have a number of choices. You may prefer that he doesn't come near the table during dinner and want to keep it that way. No problem! It's your house and your house rules. On the other

COMMON HOUSEHOLD DANGERS

Many things in your home can kill or seriously injure your dog. Consider the following:

Houseplants - see appendices for details.

Antifreeze - Sweet and deadly.

Chocolate - potentially lethal.

Bones that splinter such as chicken bones or lamb bones.

Electrical wires - can kill a puppy fast. These should be taped and tucked away.

Small choking hazards - these should be removed from environment.

Open windows, balconies and decks with wide spaced railings.

String, yarn and pantyhose can get entangled in their digestive tract. If any of these items are coming out your pup's rear end, do not pull, but go the vet immediately.

See the appendices for more detailed information regarding household dangers.

hand, some people may like their dog nearby, as I do, in which case it's a good idea to teach the next step in table manners.

The first thing to teach him is that if you invite him into your critical eating zone and he lays down quietly at your feet a nice stream of goodies will automatically come to him. Simply start reinforcing short bursts of downs at or near your feet (see pp.158 & 173 for information on teaching this command and p.211 for the proper sequence in which to introduce these concepts). If the pup gets up quickly put him back in his down position (keeping your foot on his leash is another way to encourage the pup to maintain

FOOD FOR THOUGHT

A popular myth that has been bandied about for decades is that dogs should only eat dog food and that human food is somehow bad for them. I can't help but think that this is a ploy that has been perpetrated on the public by the dog food industry. My wife's family dog grew up never tasting dog food. Whatever mom was cooking for dinner was what the dog got. The dog lived to be nineteen years old. Now I'm not suggesting that you should feed your dog pizza for dinner every night. That wouldn't be good for anyone. My wife's family, being of Hispanic descent, had some permutation of rice, beans, meat and vegetables for dinner every night. This was a diet that seemed to work pretty well for old Puffy as well as the rest of the family.

I always wondered how heavily processed and chemically preserved foods could be better for a dog than real meat and grains and vegetables. The fact is they're not. There is a great deal of nutritional information out these days about alternatives to feeding your dog commercial dog foods. This information ranges from the analysis and availability of premium high quality dog foods to recipes for cooking for your dog. Getting familiar with at least some of this data will help you make informed decisions about your dog's diet.

The following books are excellent sources of information on health and feeding alternatives for your dog: Dr. Pitcairn's Complete Guide to Natural Health for Dogs and Cats; Natural Nutrition for Dogs and Cats (Kymythy Schultze); Natural Food Recipes for Healthy Dogs (Carol Boyle); and Home Prepared Dog and Cat Diets (Donald Strombeck). These titles should be available from Direct Book Services. They can be reached at 800-776-2665 Monday thru Friday, 7:30 a.m. to 4:00 p.m. Pacific Time or at www.dogwise.com.

All that having been said I would urge you to stay with the food your pup was eating when he came from the breeder until you can get at least the rudiments of a housebreaking program put together (changes in diet can be a tad tumultuous for your pup's digestive system). When you do change foods be sure to do it gradually over the course of several weeks to allow your pup's system to adapt to the new formula.

his down) and once he's held it for a while reinforce him again with a little tidbit from your plate. Periodically command the pup to leave the area using the "out" command just to keep him honest and after some time invite him to your side once more. You'll be amazed how quickly he will absorb this routine and automatically not only find his place at your feet come dinner time but maintain a calm presence there without pestering you. He will understand that good things come to those who wait.

As your pup gets older and more familiar with all this it's fun to teach him other cute little tricks that he can perform to amuse both of you at the dinner table but again, repeatedly test the eating zone concept to always be sure that your pup continues to understand that he's not entitled to your food but rather gets it only through your good graces. Remember, you're a benevolent dictator, not a push over.

My own dog has learned all this so well that she can be up on the sofa (yes, I let her on the sofa also) with me while I'm eating my dinner there. I'll take two or three bites and give her one, take a few more, give her another one and so on. Now, if for some reason I need to leave the sofa I simply get up, set my plate down next to her and leave. Because I've taught her the eating zone concept, and respect and propriety in general, so well, she wouldn't dare touch my food and never has (I wouldn't say it never occurred to her but so far she's chosen to err on the side of caution). Because of this mutual level of trust and respect we can have our cake and eat it too and with a little practice you will be also.

Raiding food off counters and tables

Counter surfing is a favorite activity of both pups and older dogs. And who can blame them? After all, it's a fun game that produces not only the activity and excitement of the search (or hunt, in the pup's watered down wolf mind) but a major positive payoff when the ham sandwich, piece of chicken, cracker with cheese or whatever is found and promptly devoured. While it might be great fun for your pup the problems this behavior poses for you are obvious. A dog that surfs counters or table tops has to be locked up when dinner is being prepared or anytime food is out either for yourselves or guests. This

A PLACE AT DINNER

If you prefer not to have your pup ever come to the dinner table while you're eating you can teach him to go to his own place for dinner. Each night at dinner time simply tie him down nearby, providing him with both a comfy bed and something wonderful to chew on like a stuffed Kong Toy, a juicy bone (big beef bones only, no chicken, lamb or pork as these splinter), or anything else that he really loves. As you guide him to his dinnertime tie-down issue a command such as "place." What you'll find is that after some period of time, when he sees your dinner plates coming out, he'll simply take himself to his place and you'll be able to fade out the tie down. He'll also learn to go to his bed when issue the "place" command.

represents a major limitation on your pup's future activities and could prevent a full integration of his life with yours. Therefore it's important to teach him right from the start that this is a major no-no.

In order to do this set him up. That is, create a situation that is guaranteed to make your pup give it a whirl so you can be right there to teach him what happens when he does. Go and get an armful of the most tempting items you can find such as cheese, hot dogs, chicken or anything else delicious that your pup will find irresistible and lay it temptingly out on the table. Then position yourself nearby, seemingly unaware of the pup's thoughts and motivations, with squirt bottle in hand. When you see that your pup is approaching the food and is within say six to twelve inches of it with clear intentions, simply explode on him. Scream bloody murder, squirt him in the mouth and chase him down the hallway, causing him to run for his life. I mean it! This should be a psychologically shocking experience for your pup, one that he should seek to avoid at all costs in the future. To see if it has been sufficiently memorable leave the food out the rest of the day and see if he'll give it another shot. If he does, double the intensity of your reprimand. Pretty soon your pup will become paranoid about approaching items on the coffee table and that's just fine. Because the temptation to grab something so readily available in your absence is so great there must be an even greater aversion to doing so. Despite how drastic it may sound, causing your pup to be a bit superstitious about the bad things that happen to counter surfers is a good thing.

Once you've gone through this several times in one place, set up the same situation in different parts of the house at different times of the day. You don't want your pup to think that this new law only applies on the coffee table in the living room on Saturday mornings, but not on the dresser in the bedroom on Tuesday afternoon, or on the kitchen counter on Friday night.

ENTRAPMENT!

If you want to teach your puppy that a certain behavior is always unacceptable you shouldn't just wait for the undesired event to happen. You should create a situation that will all but guarantee that your pup will behave in a way you don't want him to. That's right. In this manner you assure that you'll be ready to send your pup the exact message you want: don't do that again!

It's too easy to let the pup slide here and there simply because you weren't prepared to reprimand the behavior right at the moment. This teaches him that sometimes the behavior has a payoff and thus he learns to weigh and measure. The longer this is allowed to go on the more persistent the behavior will become.

On the other hand, if you create many set-ups over a relatively short period of time the pup will quickly conclude that the behavior never has a payoff and cease and desist, usually permanently.

During the time that you're teaching your pup about the horrible side effects of counter surfing, it's important that you never let him have another successful raid. If you do it will set your training back significantly as your pup figures out that there is sometimes still a payoff and he learns how to weigh and measure. Preventing another successful raid shouldn't be a problem if you're diligently supervising as described in the housebreaking section and it shouldn't take more than a few weeks of this treatment before your pup just puts stealing food out of his mind.

The trap built - penny laden cans.

If you've been less than diligent in preventing counter surfing and have a crafty and daring pup who's figured out that he should wait until you're nowhere to be seen before any raids are attempted you'll have to convince him that you're more crafty than he. In other words, you have to booby trap him. There are any number of ways to do this but I'll give you my favorite. Make a few shake cans (empty soda cans with five or six pennies in each and a piece of tape across the top to keep them from falling out) and tape a long piece of sewing thread to each can. Then get some bait, bagels with cream cheese are my favorite, tie the other end of the threads to it and set it temptingly on the edge of some surface. Be sure to do this in such a way that the cans are as out of sight as possible and at the thread's full extension. Once the trap is set leave the room and grab a throw pillow or some other soft, bulky item.

The trap set - tied to a bagel.

Now you'll have to lie in wait but when your pup goes for the bait you'll know it immediately because you will hear the cans come rattling down. Now, for many pups the noise of the cans tumbling down around their ears is sufficient to scare the daylights out of them, however, for many others it isn't. That's why there's a second part to this trap. The moment you hear the cans hit the floor, from wherever you are in the house, start issuing loud reprimands, charge into area and throw the pillows at the pup (Gently please, just enough to startle. Remember, the point isn't to hurt him, or, as I said before, the idea is not to be mean, but meaningful).

Once again, chase him down the hallway and have him running for his life. Of course, if your pup is very shy you should scale all this back a bit.

In this exercise it's extremely important to start verbally reprimanding your pup *the moment the cans hit the floor.* Why? Remember a while back I said that you can only reprimand your pup for what he's doing at the moment you reprimand him, and definitely never after the fact? If you hear the cans come down, say nothing, charge into the kitchen and get the pup with the pillows, depending on how long it took you to get there, your pup might not be entirely clear on why he's being reprimanded. After all, it might have been five seconds since the original infraction and by the time you get there he's already backed away from the bait. In this case the whole thing wouldn't make any sense to him. However, by beginning your verbal reprimand the second the cans hit the floor *and continuing to reprimand him* until the pillow launch you are building a bridge back to the original behavior. In other words, even if the pillows from hell came five seconds after the fact your pup will know that all the trouble started the moment he grabbed the bagel and will see the entire sequence as one event.

IT'S AN ILLUSION

Throughout the course of your pup's life you're going to want to have him labor under a whole host of illusions. First among these is that you're always in control. It's through the creative use of set-ups and a dedication to consistency that this illusion is created. Once it is created your dog will assume it's always true and rarely, if ever, challenge you or get himself into trouble.

As with the above exercise, you should practice this in different locations at different times of the day until your pup is no longer tempted to go on counter surfing expeditions. My experience has been that three seems to be the magic number. That is, most pups generally give the entire habit up after three effective episodes of entrapment. Please keep in mind that, as I've already mentioned, a corollary to both of these exercises is that you supervise your pup at all times and never let him have another opportunity to have a successful raid. The trick is to convince him that this is a behavior that always only has a negative payoff. If your negative payoffs are interspersed with positive payoffs the behavior will never completely subside. You'll simply teach your pup to weigh and measure and become more cunning in his raids.

Furniture rights

As with other house rules, there are no absolutes here. You should decide if you want your pup, and later your adult dog, on the furniture or not. If you don't ever want him on the furniture do not let him up as a pup. Not only that, but don't hold him in your lap while sitting on the furniture since that's likely to send mixed messages. Join him on the floor and snuggle with him there. If you want him to only have access to a particular piece of furniture you can teach him that by encouraging him – or even placing him there if he's too small – to get up himself. Simply deny him access to every other piece of furniture in the house. If you see him begin to climb up where he shouldn't issue a sharp verbal reprimand and quickly whisk him off whatever he's climbing on. Again be consistent and direct and your pup will learn what you want very quickly.

If you want to have it both ways, that is, sometimes have the pup on the furniture and sometimes not, teach him that he must have your permission before climbing aboard. Again, the default position here should initially be no furniture rights and when your pup has absorbed that and not challenged you for a month or more then you can give him some kind of cue, either verbal or physical, to signal permission to come up. In my own case I use a special blanket and a command. When I want my dog Zoë up on the sofa or the bed with me I get out her special blanket and lay it on the sofa. She has learned to understand this cue and then eagerly awaits the "c'mon up" command before she joins me. Of course, when I tell her to get off (usually when I hear my wife Rose, who takes a dim view of dogs on the furniture, approaching) she'll promptly depart. Once again, effective training allows you to have your cake and eat it too.

Chewing

All puppies chew, and many do it relentlessly. Like little landsharks, they're gnawing their way through your house and possessions, leaving behind them a trail of destruction that would make a White House paper shredder green with envy. This is due to the fact that they are not only experiencing various stages of teething through-out their puppyhood, but that their mouth is their primary tool for exploring their environment. Thus to expect a pup not to chew is a hopeless and futile proposi-tion and therefore you must teach him what to chew and what not to.

The best way to specifically teach your pup what not to chew is to simply follow him around with a squirt bottle and spritzing him with it in conjunction with the "off" com-mand when he starts to put his mouth on something unacceptable (see p.152 for more information on this command and p.211 for the appropriate order in which to introduce these exercises). Since you're actively supervising him when he's not confined this shouldn't be too difficult. Coating electrical cables, wooden corners and other vulnerable areas with Bitter Apple spray or cream is often also very helpful for protection during those moments when you've been, well, let's say less than diligent in your supervision efforts or for those times you need to leave him in a pen in the kitchen with some access to vulnerable areas. For those pups who seem to have a taste for Bitter Apple try putting some Vaseline on the item to be protected and then sprinkling some cayenne pepper on that. Crude but effective!

However, simply preventing your pup from chewing things you

don't want him to is less than half the answer. The bigger part of preventing this problem is to give your pup an outlet for chewing that is not only appropriate but more interesting than the things you'd rather he left alone.

There are a million chew toys for dogs out on the market today, some of them wonderful and some of them awful. Let's take a look at the awful ones first before you run out and buy them. As a first rule, try to avoid toys that resemble things in the house that you don't want your dog to chew on. Let's not make things more difficult for your pup than they already are. The worst offenders I can think of in this category are rawhide slippers and worse, actual sheepskin slippers with a squeaker in them. It should be obvious why this is a problem. How is your pup supposed to know the difference between the toy and the real thing? Along the same lines, I once had a client call me because her four-month old Tibetan Terrier had chewed up an entire corner of her expensive Oriental rug. He had started on the fringe and worked his way into the main part of the rug resulting in a costly and complicated repair. When I asked her to show me the dog's favorite chew toy she brought out one of those rope toys that has big knots on either end with fringe sticking out. "This is your problem" I told her. "How is your dog supposed to know the difference between the fringe on this three dollar toy and the fringe on your fifty thousand dollar carpet?" Things are often so obvious in retrospect.

> **DON'T ADD TO THE CONFUSION**
>
> *There are a million chew toys for dogs out on the market today, some of them wonderful and some of them awful. As a first rule, try to avoid toys that resemble things in the house that you don't want your dog to chew on. The worst offenders I can think of in this category are rawhide slippers and worse, actual sheepskin slippers with a squeaker in them. It should be obvious why this is a problem.*

Another popular dog toy that one should be careful with are those plush little stuffed squeaky toys. They often resemble pillows and cushions and again it can make it difficult for the pup to determine which toy is his and which isn't. If you're going to use toys like this I recommend that you get only one and definitely not more than two at a time and teach your pup that those two are his but nothing else that may resemble them is. Definitely don't let him have three, five, ten of those toys for then it will be too easy for him to conclude that anything soft laying around is his. This applies doubly if you have small children in the house. Child's toys and dog's toys are often dangerously similar.

What then can your dog safely chew on? Well, to start with, things that are distinctly unlike everything in your house that you don't want your pup to chew on. Kong Toys are wonderful. They are made of hard rubber, are hollow inside and have a hole in the bottom. The hard rubber hopefully does not resemble any valuables you might have in the house and is virtually indestructible. The fact that it's hollow and has a hole in the bottom allows you to stuff the toy with things like peanut butter, cream cheese, biscuits, chunks of hot dog, and many other yummy items. Because the items are difficult (though definitely not impossible) to get out they'll keep most pups entertained for quite some time. You can also buy hollow bones at the pet shop and do the same thing, that is, stuff them with food. Again, the texture and smell is entirely different from anything in your home and thus it will be difficult for your pup to draw the conclusion that he can chew on inappropriate articles. Buster Cubes and toys of that ilk are great for many dogs as well. They are cube shaped or ball shaped hollow hard plastic toys that are filled with hard treats which fall out as the dog rolls the toy around. Many dogs will find hours of entertainment in the company of such "interactive" toys. Nylabones, Gumabones, cornstarch bones or anything else that has a powerful food based attraction for your pup and is textured and shaped in a way that is completely different from anything else in your home make wonderful chew toys. Many pups that are teething also often derive great comfort and relief from ice cubes as well as frozen butcher bones. Whatever works is okay so long as it doesn't lead to confusion.

Once your pup has all his toys your challenge will be to keep him interested in them. To this end, don't leave them all out at once and scattered all over the place. Not only is this unsightly, but two things can happen. Your dog may quickly get bored of them or, if they're lying around everywhere, he might still assume that anything that's lying around is fair game, including your TV remote, glasses and dirty socks. So if you've got eight or ten things that your dog really likes put out three at a time and rotate them. Also rotate the type of treats you're putting in the Kong

EVERYONE'S AN EXPERT

The moment you get a puppy it seems that everyone you meet suddenly becomes a puppy expert. You'll be subjected to all sorts of well-intentioned and mostly ill-conceived advice regarding your new puppy. My recommendation is to smile, thank the person, and by and large ignore their advice. Or at the very least run the advice by a reliable source, that is, someone who has some actual expertise in the subject and then proceed with a course of action.

Toys, bones, etc. This will help keep your pup interested in them and avoid having toys all over the place. And last but not least, leave a "target toy" in each room that you frequent with your pup so that he's always got an appropriate place to go to relieve his need to chew.

In short, you should make the choice easy for your pup. The choice should be: chew on this. It's delicious and fun. Alternatively, you can chew on this. It smells and tastes like Bitter Apple or cayenne pepper or will lead to getting squirted. Junior won't need a degree from Harvard to figure this out.

Digging

Unlike chewing, digging is not a necessary activity for a puppy though it's undoubtedly a lot of fun. As with any other unwanted behavior you must give him important feedback about this one and once again the easiest way to do it is by reprimanding him with the squirt bottle accompanied by an "off" command (see p.152 regarding this command as well as the timeline on p.211 for the appropriate order in which to introduce these exercises). Lobbing shake cans from hidden spots is effective also and for all of this, supervision is the key.

If you find that your pup is digging in your absence you have several options. First, don't let him have access to the area unsupervised. Put him in his crate or some other doggie proofed area of confinement such as an ex-pen and keep him out of trouble. If, for some reason, you have no choice in the matter there are a number of products out on the market that you can spray in areas of your yard that you'd like to keep the pup away from. Most of these are available either in pet shops or gardening shops. Results

I'm goin' for Chinese food!

are mixed but it's worth a try. Booby trapping the holes will often work as well. If you find a hole that your pup has recently excavated fill it with a very thick layer – up to an inch – of either cayenne or ground black pepper and then cover it with just a smattering of dirt. Additionally, bait the trap with a sliver of hot dog buried just under the surface which will often attract your pup back to the scene of the crime. This time, when he starts digging, he's in for an unpleasant surprise: a mouth and nose full of pepper.

If you're uncomfortable with the pepper approach try taking a small balloon and inflating it almost to the bursting point and then burying it in the hole. Again, bait the hole with a hot dog sliver and when the pup digs the balloon will explode in his face. Finally, burying a pile of poop in the hole, though disgusting, can also be effective. All of these are called *environmental corrections* (they come from the thing itself, not from you) and teach your pup that digging itself is a dangerous activity *regardless of whether you're there or not.* Even if your pup is in the habit of digging new holes in addition to the old ones these tricks can work if the new craters are diligently booby trapped. In this manner a majority of his digging excursions will result in something unpleasant and in many cases the pup will be permanently dissuaded. Leaving out plenty of attractive chew toys such as the ones described above can also help divert the pup from his annoying digging habit by distracting him to something acceptable.

There is one additional choice. Teach your pup to dig only in a particular location. If you're in the fortunate position of having a large yard you can create a *digging pit* for your pup, that is, an area where it is appropriate for him to dig to his heart's content. Sometimes one of those child's plastic sandboxes will do just fine or if you're really ambitious you can dig a hole yourself, fill it with beach sand and teach your pup to entertain himself there. You can do this by simply burying some bones and treats in the sand, with just a slight piece sticking out, and encouraging him to nose around in there. You can even dig out a few yourself and give them to him as a means of demonstrating the idea. Once your pup catches on there's only one more thing to do. Seriously reprimand him for digging anywhere else!

BOREDOM RELATED BEHAVIOR

A lot of annoying puppy antics are the direct result of boredom, digging among them. Be sure your pup is getting ample exercise (without overdoing it) and has plenty of attractive play altermatives in an area where he might dig. These would include marrow bones, Kong Toys with cheese or peanut butter or any other toy that will attract and keep his attention. Between exercise, alternatives and booby traps you should be able to eliminate digging shortly.

Preventing Object Guarding

I recently had a very nice Rottweiler named Otis stay at my home for two weeks of boarding and training while his parents set off on a European vacation. I had known Otis since he was eight weeks old and you couldn't want a sweeter dog. There wasn't a mean bone in his heavily muscled body and he was completely tolerant of anything the three small children in his household could dish out. So imagine my surprise on Otis' first night at my home when I walked near him while he was eating and he began growling at me. I was totally shocked. After reprimanding him I immediately phoned the owners, hoping to catch them before they left on their trip, to talk to them about this. The first thing I asked was if they fed Otis alone in an isolated area. I knew the answer would be yes and indeed it was. When I informed the owner of what happened he responded with surprise: "well, he's never done that before." Of course he hadn't. Nobody had ever come near him while he was eating. Otis always got to eat alone in the garage and everyone was instructed not to disturb him. "What are you going to do if one of your kids accidentally goes near him while he's eating?" I asked. "Uh, well, I guess I don't

Mine!

ON THE LIGHTER SIDE – CANINE RULES OF POSSESSION

What's mine is mine and what's yours is mine is a dog's general theory of ownership unless otherwise instructed. The following list of dog property laws, gleaned from the Internet, pretty well sums it up.

1. *If I like it, it's mine.*
2. *If it's in my mouth, it's mine.*
3. *If I can take it from you, it's mine.*
4. *If I had it a little while ago, it's mine.*
5. *If it's mine, it must never appear to be yours in any way.*
6. *If I'm chewing something up, all the pieces are mine.*
7. *If it just looks like mine, it's mine.*
8. *If I saw it first, it's mine.*
9. *If you are playing with something and you put it down, it automatically becomes mine.*
10. *If it's broken, it's yours.*

Touch him while he's eating

know," came the reply. Clearly this is not an acceptable situation and you should work from the moment you get your puppy to ensure that he will never be protective or aggressive around food or toys of any kind.

With a young pup this is very easy to do. First, make sure not to designate a special, isolated eating zone for your pup "so he can eat in peace." Feed him in the noisiest, busiest part of your

Take his dish away

Put a treat in it

And return it

A KILLER AT THE FOOD BOWL?

Some pups, though not many, are extraordinarily aggressive around their food dish from early on. They'll snarl, growl and perhaps even lash out to bite you. Often such pups come from large litters where they literally had to fight for every bit of nourishment they received. If you have one of these pups you need to be extra diligent in pursuing the food bowl exercises outlined in this section. However, if your pup lashes out with a bite you must respond with an extremely firm reprimand immediately. **All attempts at real aggression by your pup must be dealt with firmly for if he finds even once that threats or actual acts of aggression are successful strategies at getting you to back off the behavior will skyrocket,** *often even after only one incident. A firm reprimand would include giving him a solid shake by the scruff of his neck or rolling him onto his side or back (he should be familiar with this from your handling exercises). In any case, you must persist until your pup relents. If you have the rare pup that grows increasingly aggressive as you physcially reprimand him, respond by immediately isolating him for at least an hour. As you continue to work with him your pup will learn that to threaten you is a bad idea and the food bowl exercises will teach him that he can trust around his dish, and that food is no longer a scarce resource for which he has to fight. As you imprint these elements on him you'll see the behavior diminish and disappear.*

house. This will prevent him from ever getting used to the idea that he can eat in a special zone, one which his canine instincts would encourage him to protect. Second, make sure that from day one you touch and handle your pup while he's eating. Once he's comfortable with that occasionally reach into his dish, place a treat on top of his food and remove your hand. Finally, take his dish away, place a treat on top of it and return it to your pup. These very simple steps will teach your pup not only to tolerate your presence around his dish while he's eating, they'll teach him to look forward to such occurrences because they will often produce a treat.

With regard to objects of possession you want to follow a similar routine. While your pup is gnawing on some really prized object simply go and take it from him. The moment he releases it, pop a really yummy treat in his mouth, something he's totally crazy over, and *then return his prize.* Returning the prize is the most important part of this exercise. You want your pup to feel that the entire interaction represented a net gain for him. That is, not only does he get his prize, he gets a yummy treat to boot. He should come to view this like doggie investing. He gives up his principal (the bone) for a moment, gets his interest (the treat) and then gets his principal back. All in all, not a bad deal.

Most pups will have absolutely no problem with these routines but occasionally one will test the situation with a growl or even a snap. When this happens in any circumstance, not just object guarding, you must respond *immediately and decisively.* Too many owners hesitate at this point, not being sure what to do, and let the pup get away with it. This is a potentially disastrous mistake. Your pup will have learned in that instant that threats of aggression are an effective strategy to ward off unwanted intrusions and this can cause aggressive behavior to escalate with remarkable speed. Remember that your pup is in the critical socializing period and everything you teach him during this time makes a huge impact on his psyche. Don't let him learn that aggression works. Take advantage of the fact that you are still in a position to both physically and psychologically

KEEPING OUT OF THE KITTY LITTER

Some pup's love the kitty's litter. Yuck! There are several solutions to this problem. One is to put the kitty litter in a room your pup has no access to, such as a bathroom. Drive a small nail into the door molding near the door knob and fasten a string to it. Tie the other end to the door handle and leave door open just enough for kitty to get in while keeping puppy out. If you have a tiny pup you can a put a low gate across the bathroom doorway instead so kitty can jump over it and puppy can't. Other solutions include spicing the kitty messes with Tabasco sauce, startling pup with a shake can when he gets near the litter box or elevating the litter box so the kitty can get to it but puppy can't.

dominate him and *simply explode on him* the absolute moment of the infraction. As soon as he shows the slightest signs of aggression you should firmly, and with lightning speed, grab him, roll him over on his back and pin him to the ground. Put one hand around his throat and hold it firmly *without cutting off any airflow or blood circulation* (this mimics the mouth of a higher ranking dog grabbing him by the neck, pinning him to the ground and reprimanding him), while the other hand pins his body to the ground and issue a strong reprimand in his face. Your goal should be to scare the daylights out of your pup. That's right! Believe me, if he did what he just did to you to a higher ranking dog the response would be even more dramatic. If you respond like this the very first time your pup tries to guard an object you'll most likely never have such an incident again, *especially if you continue to work with the exercises outlined above.* However, no matter how long it takes, be sure to work diligently with your pup at the earliest possible age to prevent a habit of object guarding from developing. Also, please keep in mind that I'm suggesting to do this with very young and therefore impressionable puppies. If you have an older dog that is having problems with this issue you should consult a qualified behavior expert since attempting to physically reprimand an older, more confident dog in this manner could lead to serious injuries for you.

In all of the things I've just covered – jumping up, table manners, barking, counter surfing, furniture rights, chewing and object guarding – one thing is indispensable to success: *active, diligent supervision.* If you're following the housebreaking program I outlined at the outset you shouldn't really be having a problem with this but it bears saying again. If you are not diligently supervising your pup you will not be in a position to give him the information he needs about certain activities around the house and this will make teaching house rules infinitely more difficult. Rather than learning what's okay and what isn't, your pup will learn to evade you, manipulate you and find all the holes in your system. If you reprimand him after the fact he'll also learn that you're untrustworthy and this combination of elements is not what you

want your pup to absorb during his critical socializing period because as he moves out of it he'll move into adolescence and if you think puppy hood was tough "you ain't seen nothing yet." Laying the proper groundwork during the critical socializing period gives you a solid foundation for dealing with the issues that will arise during your pup's adolescent period.

Games

I've talked about a variety of toys that are available to stimulate your pup and keep him out of trouble but I've not yet mentioned games. Games are a great way to stimulate your pup both physically and mentally, to forge a strong bond between you, and to reinforce obedience commands and other behaviors. There are a million games you can play with your pup, some good, some bad. Let's take a quick look at what makes sense and what doesn't.

First of all, you want to play games that support the overall goals that you are trying to attain with your pup which include building a confident outlook on life and viewing you as his trusted pack leader. Therefore games that run counter to these goals should be avoided. Primary in this category are chase games. I generally discourage people from engaging in games of this type because they teach your pup that you are a clumsy two-legged creature and that he is easily faster than you. This opens the door to any number of challenges and is definitely information your pup can live without. If you're already in a position with your pup where he plays "keep away" you should stop immediately. Let him drag a leash around if you must, but definitely teach him that you can always get him and never encourage chase games.

Roughhousing games are generally okay when they are played *without the pup biting*. In fact, that is what the childproofing exercise referred to above (see p.86) is all about. From the time my pup was three months old to the present day I have routinely roughhoused with her, a game that we both still enjoy. But there are a few rules. First, I *initiate the game* with the verbal cue "let's play." I don't want my pup demanding games from me, especially rough ones, and then feeling like I've complied with her wishes. Once we've begun playing I will periodically suddenly place her on her back, a position I taught her to accept early on through handling exercises and which immediately calms her down, and hold her there for a moment until the stimulation level of our play session subsides significantly. Only when she's really settled will I let her up and re-invite play. This teaches her that I *control the game*. Then we play for a while longer – hard – and I repeat this routine. If, at any point, she uses her mouth on me in even the slightest, seemingly accidental, way – this is referred to as reckless biting – I will immediately reprimand her by putting her in a submissive position, grabbing her muzzle, squeezing it shut and launching a verbal reprimand in her face as described in the section on handling exercises (p.77). Once she's settled down we resume play but if she mouths me again during that session not only will I repeat the reprimand, I will end the session. Finally, during every play session I will suddenly start issuing obedience commands (more on obedience in a moment), two or three in rapid succession, whose performance is immediately rewarded with more play. And of course, at some point, when I tire of the game *I end it*. In short, *the rules for game play are: you initiate, control, and end the game and a zero tolerance policy on biting is in place*. Played in this way even rough games reinforce your training goals, that is, teaching your pup to be respectful and attentive even during periods of intense stimulation.

To properly play tug-of-war...

Initiate the game with a...

"let's play" and go for it...

In relation to this last point I realized something early on with my pup. Whereas during our periods of roughhousing I had available not only both hands and feet but my entire body to wrestle with her, because of the no bite policy her only real tool of engagement, her mouth, had been removed. This didn't seem quite fair and I wanted to do something to satisfy her need to use her mouth in rough play. The solution that I came up with was a tug toy and this brings me directly to the next subject: tug-of-war.

Conventional wisdom has it that you should never play tug-of-war with your pup since it will likely encourage dominant behavior, especially if you let the pup win. I beg to differ. This is a half-truth. As with the roughhousing described above, playing tug-of-war is fine *if a few rules are observed.* They are essentially identical to the roughhousing rules. *First, initiate the game. Second, no biting.* In relation to tug-of-war you should make it difficult for your pup to avoid biting you by moving the toy around quickly and unpredictably in such a way that it would be easy for him to actually do so in the frenzy of play. Why? In order to teach him to be extra

After thirty to forty-five seconds command "off."

Then ask for an obedience command and then go back to playing.

careful with his mouth, no matter what he's doing. So, if your pup bites he gets an immediate reprimand, a loud "no," and the game is over for the time being. After a few moments you may resume the game and if your pup recklessly bites again he gets another reprimand and the game is over for good. Don't play with him again for at least a few hours. *Third, control the game.* Throughout the game demand random "off" commands from your pup (see p.152 for more information on this command) at thirty to forty-five second intervals upon which your pup is to *immediately* release the toy. If he fails to comply he gets squirted with your handy squirt bottle, which is conveniently hidden behind your back or hooked in your pocket. Once your pup releases the toy give him a short string of obedience commands and the moment he complies, resume play. Throughout the game you may also let your pup win occasionally and, after a few moments of allowing him to savor his glory, demand that he release the toy with a simple "off" command. *Fourth, end the game.* (See photos on previous page). When you've finally had enough of the game simply demand an "off" and put the toy away. This should be your pup's cue that the game is over. Any further pushy demands to keep playing should be met with a firm "no" and a time out on a tie down or in a play pen if he persists.

Let's take a quick look at what your pup is learning here. He learns that you're the initiator of all the action. He learns that no matter how stimulated and worked up he is, there is never an excuse for his teeth even so much as grazing you. His "off" command becomes rock solid. He learns to drive all that play energy into the obedience commands for which you should routinely ask him (more on obedience shortly) thus significantly speeding up his responses. He also learns that obedience commands apply no matter how worked up he is and it teaches him that obedience is fun. Finally, he learns that even if you've let him win a round and make off with the tug toy he must give it up upon a simple request. Played like this the whole game directly supports everything that you're trying to do with your pup. Additionally, games like this build tremendous confidence in puppies. Properly played they teach them to be outgoing and enthusiastic without becoming pushy and demanding.

However, one caveat does exist: *if you cannot strictly adhere to these rules or if you have children who can't, do not play these games.* If you play without obeying these rules you can create exactly what so many trainers warn you about: a dominant, pushy, and possibly even aggressive dog.

Of course there are many other games you can play with your pup but you should apply the above rules to all of them. Initiate, control, ask for obedience commands and end the game at your whim. One wonderful game, perhaps more characteristic of dog ownership than any other, is fetch. While some pups are simply born to play this game other are less inclined but can be encouraged. If you'd like to build your pup's interest in this game begin by teasing him with the toy for some time, then giving him just a few throws before stopping. The important thing is to keep him wanting more and never giving him his fill. That way you can be sure that his level of anticipation and excitement over the game will rise rather than fall. Some dogs, no matter what you do, are simply not natural retrievers but there are many other games available. One of my favorite is hide and seek. One person holds the puppy while the other one hides with a pile of treats and then calls him. Help your pup out if you have to by luring him with your voice until he finds you and then reward him with a string of treats. Related to this are tracking games that teach him to find you by following your scent. There are a number of

WAYS TO ENCOURAGE FETCHING

If your pup is a bit reluctant to fetch there are a few things you can do to encourage him. First, tease him with the toy without letting him have it. Do this for some days or even a couple of weeks. This builds desire for the toy. Once he's developed a strong attraction to the toy throw it a short distance. When he brings it to you ignore the toy and pet your pup. Only after a short while take the toy and repeat. This discourages your pup from getting into a game of keep away. If he begins to try to play keep away despite this, offer him a second toy when he returns with the first one. Tease him with it until he drops the first one and then immediately throw it across his line of sight. Once he's off for the second toy, pick up the first one and repeat the procedure. Generally I try to keep treats out of retrieve games because it tends to take the pup's focus off the game and put it on the treat, quickly diminishing his interest in the toy. Good luck!

books available that teach fun tracking exercises in a positive and motivational way. Agility training is another great way to spend time with your dog and most areas have organized agility clubs. I started my pup at about four months in basic agility exercises and you can start teaching foundational elements even earlier than that. There are a million other ways to play with your pup, including tricks and often your pup will teach you new games. Just always keep the rules in mind: initiate, control, combine with obedience and end at your leisure.

In this section I've covered pretty much everything inappropriate that your pup could get into. Once again, the trick to making all this work is effective supervision. Avoid putting your pup in a position where he gets to make his own decisions, because frankly, they'll usually be the wrong ones. Instead, teach him to look to you for direction and learn the behaviors appropriate to whatever

FUN AND GAMES

There are numerous ways to challenge and entertain both your pup and yourself. The only real limitation is the amount of time you have available for such undertakings. Puppies can learn tracking exercises, endless numbers of tricks, and agility, to name just a few things. Below are a few resources you can look into if you're interested.

For tricks, take a look at the following: Carol Lea Benjamin, Dog Tricks; Dog Tricks for Dummies by Sarah Hodgson and Take a Bow...Wow, Fun and Functional Dog Tricks (video) by Virginia Broitman and Sherry Lippman.

For agility see: Agility Fun the Hobday Way: Agility Training for Puppies.

For tracking try: Fun Nosework for Dogs, by Roy Hunter and The Puppy Tracking Primer by Carolyn Krause.

Most, if not all, of these books are available from Direct Book Services. They can be reached at 800-776-2665 Monday thru Friday, 7:30 a.m. to 4:00 p.m. Pacific Time or at www.dogwise.com.

situation he might find himself in. In this way, as he gets older he will simply absorb the appropriate behaviors and forget all about the undesirable ones. This, in turn, will lead to trust and ultimately greater freedom for your dog.

Courtesy: Linda Grauer

Bacchus, a happy twelve-week old English Mastiff puppy.

Setting the Tone III or Acclimating Your Pup to Life

Introduction

So far I have examined setting the tone for your pup's relationship with you, your family and situations that take place within your home. The primary focus has been on things you don't want him to do. However, if your pup is going to have the most expansive and exciting life, one filled with all sorts of interesting possibilities, there are a great many things you're going to want him to do and be able to deal with. I'll repeat what I've said before: whatever he gets used to during the first four or so months of his life he'll probably be just fine with during the rest of his life. However, if he doesn't get used to things during that time frame he'll have an increasingly difficult time adapting to them as he gets older. There are three primary things that you must condition your pup to accept if he's to live a life free of stress and fear in an often confusing human world: people, dogs, and situations.

People

Throughout his life your pup will be exposed to literally thousands of people, people of every color, shape, size and overall appearance. If he is to take all this in stride be sure to start introducing him to as many people as possible as early as possible and as often as possible. Almost no one can resist petting a cute new puppy so simply walking outside with him (in your arms, of course, if he hasn't had all his vaccinations) is guaranteed to draw a crowd. Let anyone and everyone pet him and even give him treats during this early phase because as he gets older you'll find that less and less people will be so eager to say hello to him. This is especially true if you've got one of the more intimidating looking breeds like a Rottweiler, German Shepherd, or Doberman. As you do this be sure to include in your introductions all manner of people: Black, White, Hispanic, Asian, young, old, male and female, people with hats, canes, shopping carts and anything else your pup might interpret as odd. I can't tell you how often I get calls with owners complaining that their dog hates Asians, Mexicans, Blacks, Whites, men, children, etc. Dogs are not born racists or bigots but they can become equal opportunity offenders if they haven't been properly socialized.

What I did with my own puppy starting at about seven weeks of age was take her to the busiest parts of town

A BIG HEADS UP!

Occasionally a client will complain to me that they don't want their dog to take food from and be friendly with everyone, that they want them to be somewhat suspicious and even aggressive towards "bad people," but okay with "good people." If this is you I would seriously caution you! Your chances of having an encounter with a "bad person" that your dog will save you from are extremely slim but your chances of having an encounter with a "good person" that your dog will either threaten or outright attack due to lack of socializing are quite high and once you've crossed that line it's very difficult to come back over to the other side. Keep in mind that the best protection value of a dog is deterrence and a well-trained, well-socialized dog that you can take anywhere is much more of a deterrent than a dog you can't take anywhere because he inappropriately threatens or bites people. If your dog has to stay home because of an aggression problem his protection value to you while you're out will be exactly zero.

By the way, should your dog ever bite someone and it turns out that he's been somehow systematically trained for aggression, not only do you face a civil liability, you also face criminal liability. It's called "assault with a deadly weapon." That's a major felony. I have been called various times to make such assessments for the purposes of legal action and the impact of a positive finding is usually devastating for both dog (euthanasia) and owner (jail time). For more information about the legal ramifications of dog ownership please see Dog Law, by Mary Randolph available from Direct Book Services. They can be reached at 800-776-2665 Monday thru Friday, 7:30 a.m. to 4:00 p.m. Pacific Time or at www.dogwise.com.

during the busiest parts of the day in neighborhoods that reflected the multicultural character of the city in which I live, San Francisco. I would stand with her at five p.m. at the bus stop on the corner of Sansome and Montgomery streets in the heart of the financial district. Thousands of people would pour out of their offices after hectic and stressful days and when they saw me standing there with an eight-pound puppy in my arms they drew to us like filings to a magnet, eager to stroke the little furball. I would hand out treats to anyone who would take them and they in turn would give them to her. She, of course, thought this was a great deal of fun and could barely contain her enthusiasm as wave after wave of onlookers pressed in to get their hands on her. Of course, all the while she was also getting conditioned to the noise of busses, motorcycles, horns and the rest of the din associated with downtown rush hour. I did this particular exercise about ten times during the first four months of her life. However, I didn't stop there. In order to ensure that she didn't develop an overly strong preference for financial analyst types I would, on other days, take her into the heart of the Mission District, a vibrant, ethnically and economically mixed neighborhood where within fifteen minutes the entire mosaic of urban humanity would pass us by. We said hello to homeless people pushing carts, young toughs from the neighborhoods, little old ladies from Nicaragua, Chinese fish merchants, policemen…the list goes on. It's amazing the doors of communication a little puppy can open. Of course the general impression my pup was left with was that life is essentially a positive and multi-layered experience that poses no threats to her. In other words, she would never experience these situations as stressful or threatening and thus I could take her into any of them with complete ease.

INTRODUCING YOUR PUPPY TO:

Children - *Introduce gently and carefully teaching your child appropriate handling etiquette and your pup "no biting," (pp.75-77) And* **never** *leave your pup and your child unsupervised together!*

Cats - *Have your pup on the leash. It's helpful if he's learned the "off" command (p.152). Bring the cat(s) into the area and close off escape routes, forcing them to be together. Encourage kitty with treats and reprimand pup with "off" and a squirt for inappropriate moves on the cat. In due course they'll likely become friends (see next page for more).*

Ferrets, guinea pigs, hamsters etc. - *should be introduced in their crate to a tired pup. From there move forward slowly and as seems appropriate. Keep your squirt bottle handy!*

Older Pets - *Introduce off property if possible and don't be surprised if older dog reprimands your pup causing squeals of fear. They'll usually work it out within a few days.*

Additionally, I paid special attention to children. That is, to be sure that my pup would never have a problem with them I went out of my way to find as many as I could. The best places, of course, are parks, playgrounds, and schools just getting out. I repeated the above procedure numerous times to the sounds of squealing and giggling kids of all ages. Everyone gave her treats and made a big deal over her. She loved the attention and the interaction and to this day gets a little beside herself when she sees kids. She just loves them.

Vigorously pursuing these exercises, not only through puppyhood, but well into adolescence and even adulthood, will almost certainly assure that your pup will never have a problem with the variety of people that he might encounter during his life in the world of humans.

PUPPIES AND CATS

While for some cats a new pup in the household is no big deal, for a great many it can be shocking and both pup and kitty will take some time to get used to one another. If you find yourself in the situation where your pup is overwhelming the cat there are two things you have to do: convince your cat that your pup is safe, and make your pup safe in relation to the cat.

To this end try the following routine. Once your pup is habituated to wearing a leash (p.148) tie him to a piece of furniture in one of your rooms. Then bring the cat into the room and close the door, preventing any escape opportunities for him. Ideally you will have deprived kitty of a meal or two, ensuring that he'll be extra hungry for your training session. With both the cat and the pup in the room, and all escape routes blocked, present the cat with a bowl of canned tuna, salmon or something else utterly irresistible at a distance from the pup at which kitty will eat it. At the same time, reprimand your pup with squirts from your bottle for any moves he makes towards the cat. As both of them settle into this situation see if you can move the kitty bowl closer and closer to the pup. The goal, of course, is to have the kitty eating right next to the pup without the pup acting inappropriately. Simultaneous with this exercise you should reprimand your pup, as he's following you around the house on a leash (p.49), every time he makes a move on the cat.

While these routines work, be sure to be patient and take your time. Cats tend to take a long time to acclimate to changes in their environment. So once again, slow but steady wins the race.

City Noises

In line with the above is conditioning your pup to the sights and sounds of the city. Buses, motorcycles, backfiring cars, sirens, rollerbladers, bicyclists, grocery carts, construction sites and the million other annoying sounds of city life crowd in on us from all sides. We've all learned to tune them out, largely due to what some might consider excessive exposure, but if you shelter your pup from these things he won't have the same opportunity. During the course of socializing him with people as described above be sure to give him plenty of exposure to the racket of everyday life as well. More is better is a good motto here and soon your pup will learn to ignore even the most abrasive sounds and take all the chaos in stride.

The Shy Pup

If your pup is extremely sensitive and fearful in response to people and situations such as the ones described above you'll have to take some extra measures. Primarily these revolve around what is known in behavioral jargon as *systematic desensitization*. This is a fancy term that simply means exposing your pup to small amounts of the offending item, be it a sound, a certain type of person, or whatever, while producing something wonderful at the same time such as a delicious treat.

For example, if your puppy is terrified of grocery carts skip his breakfast one morning to ensure that he's very hungry, take him to the grocery store, stand about fifty feet away from where the carts are so your pup can see them without freaking out and begin giving him treats. Be sure to stand just outside of what I call the pup's *reactive zone*, that area where he starts to become afraid, and begin feeding him treats. As you see that he's focusing on the treats and relaxing, slowly begin to move him towards the

LITTLE BY LITTLE

I often tell my clients that in dog training progress is always made on the increment. What this means is that progress is usually not made in great leaps and bounds but in tiny little steps. Nowhere is this more true than in approaches using systematic desensitization. Ironically, working slowly for results will produce them faster than trying to rush it which will almost always set you back. Remember the tortoise and the hare: slow but steady wins the race!

grocery carts. If you see that he's becoming excessively nervous back off a little in order to acclimate him to that level of stimulation. Only when he's comfortable with any given level of the offending stimulus should you again begin to move closer. *Never push your pup beyond his fear threshold.* Make sure he stays reasonably comfortable and starts associating the distant presence of the stimulus with something positive i.e. the treat (also, please remember not to talk to your pup in soothing, cooing tones in an effort to reassure him, but to use a happy, upbeat tone to help pick up his attitude – see p.14 for more information on the shy pup). If you do this consistently your pup will sooner or later begin associating the fear producing stimulus with something positive and this, in turn, will begin to change his attitude about it. Eventually when he hears grocery carts he should look at you with joy and anticipation (or at the very least, indifference), not with fear and anxiety.

With this approach patience is definitely the order of the day. You can use systematic desensitization in relation to anything that your pup is afraid of. Just keep in mind that if you push your pup past his fear threshold you'll set the entire process back. Remember the tortoise and the hare: slow but steady wins the race.

Other Dogs

When you go to your breeder to pick out a pup you are separating him from his litter during the midst of his critical socializing period. This is fine because he'll learn to socialize with you from his earliest times but it's a potential problem because his learning to be a dog is interrupted. In other words, *nothing teaches a dog to be a dog like another dog.* It's usually at about five weeks of age that pups start relating to each other as playmates in the litter and begin developing and expressing their unique canine pack instincts. If you come and pick up your pup at around seven weeks (my favorite time) he's had two weeks of learning about doghood from his littermates. With your arrival this is abruptly interrupted. Now there's nothing inherently wrong with this as he now learns to adapt to his life with his new pack but if you wait months and months before getting him out with other pups he will have missed critical opportunities to learn how to appropriately interact with other dogs. This can often lead to serious behavior problems later on. In fact, I'd say that lack of early socialization is the single leading cause of dogs' aggression towards other dogs in later life.

In other words, just as you must socialize your pup with people as described above, you must also continue to socialize him with other dogs. It's here where pups learn about all sorts of doggie behaviors such as not only giving the appropriate physical social signals of

GETTING TWO PUPS AT ONCE

Often clients will ask me if I think it's a good idea to get two siblings from a litter so they can keep each other company. I generally discourage them because first, it's an unbelievable amount of work and can be overwhelming. But second, and more importantly, what can happen in situations like this is that the pups become more bonded to one another than to their owners. I usually recommend that they get one pup through the first year and half and then, if still interested, add the second.

If it's too late and you've already gotten two pups simultaneously you must ensure that they don't become so dependent on one another that they cannot spend time alone. Begin by making sure that the pups sleep separately (no crate sharing please) and are periodically separated throughout the day. Additionally, each owner should be sure to spend one-on-one time with each pup teaching the exercises outlined in this book. It's also a good idea if you decide to enroll your pups in a puppy playgroup (p.130) or doggie day care center (p.133) to take them on separate days. Too often pups, and later adult dogs, look to each other as reference points in novel situations and fail to develop the confidence to take on new situations alone. In other words, each dog can start to become an integral part of the other's identity to the point where neither can adequately function when alone. It's a lot of extra effort but if you want to ensure the long-term psychological well-being of your pups you should definitely commit to it.

A Note On Guarding Breeds

If you own a guarding breed such as a German Shepherd, Doberman, or Rottweiler early and frequent socialization is of extra importance. What defines a guarding breed? A higher than usual suspicion level and the willingness to back it up with a fight. In a dog like this you want to do everything you can to mitigate these drives through intense socialization lest you end up with a dog that is inappropriately aggressive when he matures.

dominance and submission but reading them as well. I can't tell you how many adolescent dogs I've seen that never learned to properly give or interpret canine body language and thus ended up in all sorts of trouble. It's also in the context of playing and being with other dogs that your pup has an outlet for biting, a natural and perfectly appropriate activity *in a canine context.* Remember, you're teaching him not to bite you so interaction with other dogs will give him an appropriate outlet for this behavior. In this context your pup will also learn bite inhibition, that is, how to bite without hurting, and how to use various levels of pressure to communicate various intentions in a way that is, once again, perfectly appropriate in a canine context. What brings a bit of urgency to the issue of early puppy socialization is that if a dog has not learned bite inhibition by the time he is about four and a half months old *he will never be able to learn it.* The upshot of this, of course, is that if he should at some point decide to bite he will often do so with uninhibited force.

Because of all this I am a strong advocate of early and frequent interactions between your puppy and as many other dogs as possible. However, in so doing you run headlong into the veterinary injunction to keep your pup away from any other dogs or even areas where other dogs have been until he has had all his vaccinations, usually around four months of age or the end of the critical socializing period, in order to avoid picking up parvo and other nasty little doggie bugs. While this might be sound health advice it is absolutely horrible behavioral advice. So what are you to do? Listen to your vet or to your behaviorist. Well, thankfully it's possible to find a compromise that will satisfy both requirements.

Puppy Play Groups

Most cities and even small towns these days have what is commonly referred to as puppy kindergarten, or puppy playgroups. Generally the pups in these groups are quite young, usually between eight weeks and about four months of age, and it's required that they all have at least two sets of vaccinations in before they can join the activity. In other words, the health status of all the pups there is a known quantity and no one is at risk of infection. Joining a group like this meets the veterinary safety criteria and the behavioral socialization criteria and provides the best of all possible worlds for your pup.

Primarily what happens in these groups is simply puppy play. That is, one hour of uninhibited free for all fun. Training is secondary. Often there will be ten or fifteen pups speeding around the room like little Tasmanian Devils, chasing, tumbling and essentially spinning out of control. What fun! The owners just stand around and watch, amazed at the antics of their precious little bundles. While rough dog play can sometimes make new owners nervous, nothing could be better for your pup. Not only does he come home thoroughly exhausted – and, after all, tired dogs are good dogs – he's learning everything he needs to learn about being a dog. In addition it also gives you an opportunity to observe his social interactions and nip any potential behavioral problems in the bud (so to speak).

Courtesy: Mary Watson

Let's take a moment to talk about how to handle your pup in a play group like this. For the most part you'll find that the pups will just tear around all over the place tackling each other, getting tackled, being submissive or dominant depending on the situation they find themselves in and so forth. During these times the best thing you can do is nothing at all. Simply let the dogs be dogs. They'll learn more from each other about what it means to be a dog than you could possibly ever teach them.

However, there are some times when you should be proactive. If you see that your pup is relentlessly pushing a helpless puppy around or is ganging up with one or more pups to do the same you should intervene. You don't want to create a bully in these playgroups. If you suspect that your pup might be a little too rough in the way he's relating to another pup try a simple experiment. While he's in the midst of his pushy behavior grab him by the collar or the scruff of his neck and pull him off his victim. If the other pup runs for his life you know that yours was being a bit too rough and you should direct him to other pups that are more his equal. If he continues to pursue the pup which just ran away you should follow him with a squirt bottle and spray him in the mouth while commanding "off" when he tries to pounce on him again. You're his leader and have the right to tell him "enough is enough." On the other hand, if the pup that was on the bottom, rather than running for his life, comes back for more, by all means let them have at it. Clearly everyone is having fun. Along the same lines, if you're the owner of the puppy getting pushed around don't be shy about pulling the other pup off yours to see what your pup's response is. All in all, though, resist the temptation to run to your pup's rescue every single time he gets a little overwhelmed otherwise he'll never learn to fend for himself.

SOCIALIZING THE SHY PUP

If a pup is shy early on and is never socialized it is pretty much guaranteed that he will become aggressive toward other dogs as he gets older. Not only that, but since he's never had the opportunity to learn about bite inhibition when he does bite it will often be severe. Therefore, if you have a shy pup the imperative to socialize him early and often is even greater than with any other pup.

If you happen to be the owner of a shy puppy (see p.14 for more on shy pups) who is clearly intimidated by the whole playgroup scenario there are a few rules you might want to follow. Try sitting on the floor near the edge of the playgroup with the puppy in your lap, a safe island for him to watch the goings on. If he's expressing fearfulness absolutely *do not comfort or reassure him in any way.* This will quickly make his fearfulness worse. Simply allow him to sit there in the safety of your lap. If you need to you can move further away from the area of activity until your pup is less nervous. If your pup is not in your lap but is hiding in a corner or under a chair, the same rules apply. The best thing you can do is simply ignore him. As time goes by most pups will venture out carefully, finding themselves attracted to perhaps only one other pup in the whole group. That's okay. Let him take his time. If other dogs approach your pup while he's in your lap or hiding out elsewhere and he snaps at them that's okay too. He's allowed to tell other dogs he's not interested. *However, if he gets emboldened and moves towards the other dogs in order to strike out preemptively he should be reprimanded with a quick squirt from your bottle or a muzzle grab as learned in the handling exercises* (see p.77).

Generally what will happen with even the most shy pups is that after a few sessions, usually three to six, they will learn that nothing is going to harm them here and begin to come out of their shell. Now they will have the opportunity to learn how to be dogs. *If a pup is this shy early on and is never socialized it is pretty much guaranteed he will become aggressive towards other dogs as he gets older.* Not only that, but since he's never had the opportunity to learn about bite inhibition when he does bite it will often be severe. Therefore, if you have a shy pup the imperative to socialize him early and often is even greater than with any other pup. Remember, you have a very narrow window of opportunity to vigorously and effectively socialize him before his attitude towards life begins solidifying. Take advantage of it!

Doggie Day Care Centers

A relatively new phenomenon in today's busy world are doggie day care centers. Generally these are places where one can drop off a dog in the morning and pick him up at night. Most of them only take dogs once they've had all their shots in and thus are past their critical socializing period however, some do have special puppy programs that help the pup get the social experience it needs during this time.

If you are planning to use a doggie day care center I would not discourage you however there are a few things to be aware of. First, *do not get your puppy used to being in a day care center as a daily routine.* This overly high level of stimulation as a steady diet can, with some dogs, lead to all sorts of behavior problems including severe separation anxiety and destructive behavior in the absence of such stimulation. Be sure your pup gets used to spending regular periods of time at home, alone (more on this in a moment). One to two days a week or even several half days at a doggie day care center until the end of your pup's critical socializing period should be plenty in order to enable your pup to reap the benefits of socialization. If you are going to leave a young pup in a day care center make sure the area is sanitized regularly, that the pups are being crate trained and housebroken while they're there, that their play is supervised in accordance with what I've described above and that they get plenty of down time each day. Puppies need sleep and lots of it. As I said a moment ago, constant over-stimulation of young pups can lead to extraordinary behavioral problems later. If the elements outlined above aren't in place at the center you're considering you'd be better off skipping this option and finding a one hour play group for your pup, even if only once a week.

A final thought on all this. Many people believe that they don't really need to socialize their dog because they've already got a dog at home. Sorry! That doesn't count. Socializing means strange and unknown dogs, which is precisely what you'll encounter when you start taking your dog out to parks, beaches or anywhere in the city.

Teaching your pup to accept time alone

I mentioned a moment ago that pups that are chronically over-stimulated at an early age are likely to develop problems with separation anxiety in the not too distant future. Let's take a moment to look into that, keeping in mind my admonition that anything you want your pup to be able to deal with as an adult dog, you should start getting him used to *now*.

I occasionally get a call from an excited new puppy owner during which they proudly announce that they've taken two months off from work in order to be able to spend "quality time" with their puppy. Others are excited because they can take their dog to work with them every day. In either case the implication is that they're going to spend lots of time with their pup. While I appreciate the sentiment and the dedication to the welfare of their pups that these clients are showing, I quickly inform them that this is potentially a *huge mistake*. Spending every moment of the day with your puppy is guaranteed to ensure enormous headaches with separation anxiety, one of the most difficult behavior problems to deal with. Please spare yourself the trouble.

In short, it is extremely important for your puppy to learn how to spend time alone. Each day he should have down time in his crate or special area with no one around. In order to make this easier for your pup to tolerate try to exercise him first – exhaustion translates easily into sleep while an overflow of energy translates rapidly into anxiety – and leave a special bone or toy in his crate *that he never gets any other time*. This will help him to build a positive connection with alone time. But time alone he must have.

I would suggest starting with two to three one hour periods a day and slowly adding to that as the pup gets older. If he complains about the periodic confinement reprimand him as discussed in the section on crate training (see p.44). The older the pup gets, the longer he should be able to tolerate being left alone. My goal for all my dogs is that by the time they're a year old they should be able to stay home in the house for twelve hours without experiencing anxiety. Not that you should subject your dog to that kind of isolation as a steady diet. That would be inhumane. But you want to be sure that in a pinch you can do it. You never know what life brings, what situation could arise that would suddenly and unexpectedly require you to be gone from home for twelve hours. It happens to me three or four times a year. While I feel bad for leaving my dog alone that long I know that she can tolerate it, basically without freaking out. The fact that she is at ease puts me at ease and makes both of our lives more comfortable.

Boarding

During the next ten to fifteen years, the period of time your pup will likely be with you, it's quite likely that you'll need to be out of town periodically. During these timeframes you'll clearly have to have someone take care of your dog. Since friends and family are not always available – and often don't do the job a professional would – chances are that at some point you'll need to avail yourself of the services of a kennel. Fortunately today there are many kennels that do not fit the old stereotype of dingy places with dirty runs where the dogs are essentially jailed while you're gallivanting around Europe. Quite the contrary, most cities today have kennels run by caring animal lovers where the dogs are free to play with other dogs during the day or sniff around the property and generally have a good time. I suggest you try and find a place like this for your pup early on and begin to get him used to boarding there as soon as possible. Once again, whatever you want your pup to be able to deal with as an adult dog, begin introducing it *now*.

See ya next week!

The first time I boarded my pup she was three and a half months old and had just finished all her shots (including the bordatella or kennel cough vaccination without which you shouldn't board your pup). Since my life involves a good bit of traveling I decided to follow my own advice and begin boarding her. I found a place I liked and left her there for two days. Three weeks later I repeated the procedure but left her for four days. *Keep in mind, I wasn't traveling at the time.* I only wanted to condition her to the kennel early on and teach her to understand that occasionally she'd have to stay elsewhere and that that's okay.

After about the third visit she started to view this place as her home away from home. When we'd get within a block or so of the kennel she'd start bouncing around in the car with seemingly boundless enthusiasm. This was not only the best possible endorsement the kennel could get but also let me know that I'd never have to worry about her mental health and well-being while I was enjoying my travels. Since then I've left her there literally dozens of times and aside from occasionally missing her have never had to give her a second thought while my wife and I were enjoying our trip. Boarding your dog early and often can give both you and your pup the same peace of mind.

Grooming

My dog is a Standard Poodle, a breed not only known for it's extraordinary intelligence and sense of humor, but it's grooming needs as well. Poodles need grooming every six weeks or so since their coat does not shed, a laborious process that involves bathing, blow drying, hair cutting, ear cleaning and nail trimming. Knowing that my pup would have to endure a lifetime of this type of handling I decided to condition her to it from day one. Even if your pup will not have the intensive grooming needs of a Standard Poodle it is inevitable that at some point you or someone else will have to give him a bath, a toweling off, perhaps a blow drying, brushing and nail trim. So let's take a look at how you can introduce such potentially annoying handling to your pup at an early age and perhaps even teach him to enjoy it.

Bathing

The best way to ensure that your pup will hate being bathed is to simply turn the cold water on him the first time he's dirty. Even if you don't have a full blown freak out on your hands you can pretty much guarantee that henceforth when he sees the hose coming he's going to run for his life. If you want to teach him to be tolerant of bathing introduce it early, gently and in small increments.

From the day you get your pup play games with him in and around the bathtub. Teach him that the bathroom is a place where a good time is had. Place him in the tub with no water it, roll his favorite toy around in there and, if available, bring the entire family in to shower him with attention and treats. Once

Splish Splash, I was takin' a bath!

he's become used to this and anticipates a good time, fill the tub with half an inch of *warm* water and repeat the procedure. After some initial hesitation your pup should begin to frolic and splash around in the little puddle you've made for him. As he continues to get used to and enjoy this routine add a little more water day by day. During this time you can even take a small cup, dip it in the water and pour it over him in order to condition him to the sensation of water flowing over him and of being wet. During the course of all this be sure to handle and massage him a lot – as you'll have to when you ultimately shampoo him – and provide lots of treats and affection throughout. Keep doing this until you've managed to get your pup thoroughly wet, shampooed and rinsed off. Then, of course, you'll have to condition him to being toweled off but this shouldn't be too much trouble since your pup will most likely get a small thrill out of this sensation.

Be sure to take your time with all of this and move forward only in small increments which your pup is able to handle without any upset. If you see that you've moved ahead too fast backtrack to the last level with which he was comfortable and work more slowly. Any traumatizing him will only set your efforts back. Of course, the more you do this the faster your pup will become accustomed to it and the younger and smaller he is the easier he'll be for you to handle.

Drying

Since most dogs, like most humans, find the sound of a hair dryer at least mildly annoying it is usually necessary to introduce this in small increments as well. Begin by having the hair dryer on a low setting far enough away from your pup so it does not bother him. Then start feeding him treats in the proximity of the hairdryer but never so close as to make him nervous. Continue to lure him closer as he's able to handle it. If at any point he appears anxious let him back off a little and get comfortable again.

A GREAT ONLINE RESOURCE

www.dogfriendly.com - a website for resources like hotels etc. that are friendly to dogs.
www.dogfriendly.com/server/magazine/ is a subsection of this site which contains articles on all sorts of things such as an accommodation spotlight; attraction/event spotlight/outdoor restaurant spotlight; and more. Dog friendly employers, dog friendly apartments nationwide, and much more is covered. Excellent resource!

Slowly but surely your pup will come to associate that annoying dryer sound with treats and thus learn not only to ignore it but even develop a positive attitude towards it. With my own pup I did all of this and then added one more fun exercise: the trail of treats.

Photo: Robert Polzer

I set the hair the dryer on the ground and turned it on a low setting. Then, starting about six feet away, I placed a trail of little of hot dog slivers and cheese in one inch increments leading right up to the dryer. Around the dryer itself I placed a ring of treats and for the icing on the cake I put a bunch right on top of it. No hungry puppy could resist this kind of temptation. Working with these two exercises it took my pup all of about three days to associate the sound of the dryer with great fun and come running when she heard it.

Manray, a little Lhasa

Once your pup becomes accustomed to the sound and proximity of the dryer it's time to actually let him experience the sensation of it blowing on him. Again, introduce this in small increments. Begin with the dryer on a low setting with a moderate temperature. You want to be sure that you don't burn him with the hot air. Hold the dryer at some distance away from your pup while at the same time giving him hot dog treats. Slowly keep moving the dryer closer to the pup. If you sense any tension on the puppy's part back off a little and gave him some space to relax. With my own pup, after several weeks of this type of treatment on a daily basis she had no problems whatsoever with being dried, a fact for which my groomer, I'm sure, is grateful.

Of course, simultaneous with this you should work on the bathing routine outlined above. When the day finally comes that you have to give your pup a full blown bath he should be totally accustomed to every element of these routines and everything should dovetail nicely. Of course, as time goes by and your pup gets totally habituated to all of this you can simply fade treats away and reward him at the end of the bath with a fun play session.

Nail Clipping

Nail clipping is another activity that most pups need some help getting accustomed to. As with everything else, this takes some patience and a systematic approach. Begin by simply handling his toes. This is something you should be doing with him in the context of the handling exercises outlined earlier (see p.77). Once your pup is okay with having his feet handled begin touching his toes with the nail clipper, being sure to give him a treat each time after doing so. Soon the pup will simply view the clippers as a precursor to a treat.

Then pick a time when your pup is exhausted and half-asleep and begin to clip a few nails. Gently take a paw, push out a nail and clip a tiny piece, perhaps a sixteenth of an inch, off the end. You must be very careful to clip only in very small increments in order to avoid cutting the "quick." This is a small blood filled area within the nail laden with delicate nerve endings and blood vessels (Throughout this process it's a good idea to keep some styptic powder nearby so that in the event that you unintentionally cut the quick you can stop the bleeding immediately). Of course, after each clipped nail quickly give your pup a treat. Once he relaxes again try clipping another, and so on. There's no need to clip all twenty nails at once so if you feel you've made pretty good strides with three or four you might leave the rest for the next day. Once you've got all the nails clipped I would encourage you to continue with the desensitization routines and perhaps put your pup through one more round of actual clipping before taking him to a groomer or vet to do the same. In this manner he'll have had plenty of exposure to such handling and will be likely to accept it from others with no problems.

Visiting the Groomer

The exercises outlined above should all be done in your home prior to your puppy's first visit to a groomer. If he has been properly conditioned he will be unlikely to have any problems when the groomer begins to handle him in ways you've already taught him to accept. In addition, if you've been teaching your pup to both handle time by himself and to board occasionally, suddenly being separated from you in a strange place for a half day or longer won't be such a big deal.

But there's one more thing you can do to make sure that the transition to the groomer is a seamless one: *introduce him to the groomer several times before you actually leave him there.* You can start by stopping in, having the staff give him treats and play with him for a few minutes and then leaving. Once you've done this a few times you might even consider leaving him there for an hour or so and letting him hang around without being groomed. A good groomer will cheerfully participate in these exercises with you since he or she is going to be the one having to deal with your pup. In other words, they've got a vested interest in everything working out well. In this manner, when the big day does finally come and you leave your dog for his first appointment it should be very anti-climactic for everyone involved.

Riding in the Car

As with everything else covered so far, car rides are something you should introduce early and often. This is intended not only to put your pup at ease in the car but to teach him basic manners as well. An out of control pup in the car endangers everyone in it.

Let's start by reviewing a few basic rules about car rides. First, never ride with your pup in your lap. It's extremely dangerous for both of you. Being distracted by your pup could lead you into a traffic accident, and being wedged between you and the steering wheel is seriously hazardous to your pup's health. Please do not

substitute your puppy for an airbag. Second, for similar reasons don't allow the pup to run freely around the passenger seat. Your distraction level makes driving unsafe and even a mild fender bender could turn your puppy into a projectile. Third, having your puppy unrestrained in the back seat is similarly suspect for all the same reasons.

The best place for your puppy while you're driving is in a crate in the backseat or, if you have an SUV or station wagon, in the cargo compartment. In either place you don't have to worry about what your pup is getting into and in the event of an accident he's somewhat protected. In order to keep your pup settled down it's often helpful to give him a really great chew toy such as a "Kong Toy" with peanut butter in it or a fresh knuckle bone. Keeping your puppy confined and somewhat focused in this manner teaches him that the car is not a place for wild explorations but a place for settling down and focusing on something calming. Most pups will get used to this idea rather quickly and grow up being just fine in the car.

CAR SICKNESS

If your pup has a tendency to get carsick, start by taking him for short rides around the neighbhorhood or perhaps even just up and down your driveway. Be sure to have positive experiences on either end of the trip such as some treats or a fun game. And definitely be sure never to comfort and stroke him if he's feeling ill because it will make the behavior worse.

However, some pups have a really difficult time with car rides, getting nervous and carsick even at the thought of a ride somewhere. This is understandable when you consider that the pup's first few experiences in a car usually revolve around somewhat less than thrilling events. He probably experienced his first ride when he'd just been plucked from his litter, separated from his pack and deposited in a strange new world – your home. His next trip was likely to the vet for shots as was the trip thereafter. So far not the best set of associations. If, in addition, you live along a winding road this could make matters even worse. Occasionally, because of this set of circumstances, some pups develop serious anxiety problems at the mere thought of entering a car. Often they'll drool and ultimately vomit during the ride and, of course, each time they go through this their phobia becomes more deeply entrenched.

Unfortunately dealing with a puppy that hates car rides and gets carsick is a time consuming and difficult affair and there are no short cuts. You must slowly help your pup build positive associations with rides in the car. You can start with simple exercises such as feeding, playing with or giving treats to your pup in or even near the car, with the car turned off, depending on his level of sensitivity. If you've had to start near the car, work slowly towards getting him to actually eat, play or take treats inside it. Once he's okay with this try turning the engine on and letting the car idle while he's eating. If at any point he becomes anxious or hesitant back off to whatever previous level he was at ease with.

Once he's become habituated to eating or playing in the car with the engine idling try driving just to the end of your driveway and back. Once that's okay drive back and forth up your driveway a few times. Be sure to keep the killer treats coming and eventually try to focus him on a special toy – again, a "Kong Toy" with peanut butter can be pretty persuasive.

When he's comfortable with this routine try a very short drive, perhaps to a local park or a neighbor's house, where your puppy should be immediately exposed to something irresistibly fun like a run around the grass or a play session with the neighbor or his dog (if all his inoculations are up to date, of course). Once concluded put your puppy back in the car, return home and do something special for him there. An extraordinarily positive experience on either end of the ride will do wonders for his attitude. Keep working with this routine adding distance and time *only in very small increments* and most often you'll find that your pup will begin to tolerate and perhaps even enjoy car rides. And, remember, be patient! As with other exercises of systematic desensitization, please keep

RULES OF THE ROAD

Car rides will be a regular part of your pup's life but there are a few rules to follow.

1. Never leave your pup in the car with the windows closed. Cars heat up in no time and can kill your pup in a hurry. Open your sunroof, crack all the windows, use a window shade and leave pup home on hot days.

2. Never have your pup in the front seat. An airbag can kill him.

3. Keep an extra set of keys in the glove compartment. That way, if you're caught on a hot day you can turn on the engine and A/C and still lock your car, keeping your pup cool and safe.

4. Don't let your pup stick his head out of the window. Not only can this cause eye infections, loose gravel and other road debris can take out an eye in an instant.

in mind to work at your pup's pace not the pace at which you'd like to see progress. If you push your pup past his fear threshold you'll only set yourself back.

Finally, if none of these things seem to be helping even marginally, speak to your veterinarian about doggie motion sickness pills. New medications designed to assist with dog behavior problems are coming out all the time and the best place to get this information is from a well-informed and up to date veterinarian.

The above exercises are designed to enable you to integrate your puppy into your lifestyle. The alternative is living your life around your pup and this, more often than not, results in great frustration. For example, I recently worked with a very nice couple who had a little Cairn Terrier puppy but who simply couldn't bring themselves to exert any discipline or structure on him. "We just want him to be his own dog" they insisted and despite paying me a lot of money they took practically none of my advice. Since they couldn't bear to leave their little pup alone they now only take trips which involve their dog. Rather than going to the movies, they rent videos. Rather than going out to dinner, they order in. "It's frustrating" they confessed to me a year later, "but we made a commitment to this dog and we're willing to live with it." Well, I'm sorry, I love dogs as much as the next guy but that's just nuts! You should be able to have a dog that is seamlessly integrated into your lifestyle and is an enhancement to it rather than an oppressive limitation. Being diligent in the practice of what we've covered so far will ensure that that's the case.

TEACHING YOUR PUP TO TAKE THE STAIRS

Learning to go up and down the stairs can be an intimidating experience for your puppy, especially if you have the kind of stairs that can be seen through and underneath. Try luring your pup down the stairs with a treat. If he hesitatates, begin by putting him two stairs away from the bottom and luring him from there. If he's still not sure, put one hand under his belly and help him down step by step, rewarding on each one with a treat. Once he's okay with two stairs try three, then four and so on. Pretty soon he'll catch on.

Setting the Tone IV
Beginning Obedience Training

Introduction

There are still a great many people out there, professional trainers included, who will tell you with full confidence that you can't teach your pup meaningful obedience commands until he's about six months old. *Nothing could be further from the truth!* Your pup is learning all the time, and never with more acuity and receptivity than during his critical socializing period. The real question is: what are you teaching him?

If a person on the street tells you that you can't train a young puppy it's only because they don't know any better. However, if a professional trainer tells you the same thing what he or she is really saying is, "I use relatively aggressive, harsh and compulsive methods for training and your dog will be neither physically nor psychologically cut out to handle this type of treatment until he's about six months old." In other words, you've got a big red flag.

Sit-Stay!

The truth is, you should start training your pup almost as soon as you get him. Like I said, he's learning all the time. By the time he's six months old he should be about two thirds trained. That is, he should have really solidly internalized the bulk of the behaviors he'll ultimately end up performing and your job at that point should be primarily to proof him against increasingly higher levels of distraction.

The really good news in all this is that you can do most of this training with almost no force and compulsion and build such a solid foundation that when the time does come that some compulsion is called for (it usually does) it will be minimal.

THE TREAT CONTROVERSY

Today's training world appears to be split into two conflicting factions: those who oppose the use of treats in training and those who advocate it. Those who oppose object primarily because they claim that if you use treats the dog will never obey without them. "He should do it because you said so and for your praise," is the sum and substance of the argument. No offense, but that's absurd.

First, the goal of training with treats is not to cause the dog to be forever dependent on them. It's to introduce the training concepts without physical compulsion and once grasped to fade the treats away. Second, the problem with verbal and physical praise, especially with a young pup, is that usually the pup is being petted all the time for no other reason than that he's cute. The point of praise, of course, is to highlight the moment the pup got something right. If he's being petted all day long he'll have a hard time differentiating your affection for getting a command right from the rest of what he's getting for no reason whatsoever. Using a treat allows you to precisely identify a moment of success for your pup with something special that he'll take note of.

Also in working with a young pup we want to imprint on him that training is a fun, cooperative venture and not necessarily a confrontational and adversarial process. For instance, the conventional way of teaching a dog to sit is to put a choke chain around his neck and pull straight up while pushing his rear end into the ground and saying "sit." When the pup complies the physical discomfort ceases and that's how he learns. This seems inherently unfair. The pup is being physically punished or at least made uncomfortable for something he doesn't even know how to do. Why not simply lure him into a "sit" with a treat and positively reward him when he gets it right? This allows him to use all of his mental capacity to solve the problem of how to get the treat rather than worry about why he's being pushed around. Once the behavior is well established it's a simple matter to fade treats out.

Finally, I'm not so naïve as to think that your pup will never require physical force to perform a behavior he knows how to do. That's why I've introduced handling exercise #4 (p.82) which prepares him for being physically handled into positions he'll learn how to perform with treats first. In the pages that follow you'll also learn how to introduce compulsion on the leash (p.201) but again this will only apply to behaviors that you've taken the time to introduce with treats.

In short, I cannot think of any good reason why you shouldn't use treats in training your pup but I can think of plenty why you should.

Below I will outline a beginning training program that will take your pup to what I feel he should be able to perform by the end of his critical socializing period, which is the scope of this book. By the time you're through with this you'll not only be amazed at how fast your pup can learn, you'll also have hands on experience with a sensible training approach. This experience will allow you to pick a suitable trainer or training class

A NOTE ON COLLARS AND LEASHES

Go into any pet shop and you'll find an assortment of collars, leashes and harnesses that is bewildering. Below I'll give you a couple of guidelines to get you started.

For most pups all you're going to need throughout the first four months of their life is a flat buckle collar, a six foot leash and, as he progresses in his training, a twenty-six foot retractable leash (Flexi Leashes™ are my favorite).

For most things the six-foot leash and buckle collar will be just fine. The retractable leash will be used only for recall training, as you'll see shortly. One thing is important here. Do not get into the habit of walking your pup on a retractable leash before he learns to walk nicely on a six-foot leash. If he gets habituated to having all that space from the outset he's going to have a really difficult time adjusting to the limitations of a six-foot leash. In this connection, I recommend you never walk your pup on a retractable leash through the city on sidewalks (unless it's locked at six feet) that are shared by other people. Not only don't you want him tripping everyone up with that cord, you don't want him to learn that busy sidewalks are the place for meandering excursions. You want him to learn that in such situations you want him to walk with you closely. If you habituate him like this early he'll naturally walk closely to you in the future whenever you're on a busy street. Reserve the retractable leash for places where it's okay for your pup to roam and investigate such as parks and beaches.

As far as harnesses are concerned, they're fine but don't expect to ever teach your pup not to pull a leash if he's wearing one. Harnesses encourage pulling (with the exception of specialized "no-pull" harnesses), which is precisely why they put them on sled dogs, and they make communicating with your pup through gentle nudges very difficult. I generally don't recommend them with the possible exception of tiny puppies whose necks are so delicate that a collar could be dangerous.

Finally, no puppy should ever wear a choke chain. The pressure exerted by such a collar on the sensitive, delicate and still developing neck of your pup can potentially cause serious damage. If and when training collars are used it should not be until your pup is through with his critical socializing period and well on his way to adolescence.

What If My Pup Chews The Leash?

If your pup likes to chew on his leash you have several options. The first involves simply soaking the last six inches or so of the leash with Bitter Apple™ spray. If that doesn't work Bitter Apple™ also comes in a cream that you can also apply to the leash. If your pup is one of those that actually likes this product (there are a few) put a little petroleum jelly on the last twelve inches of the leash and then sprinkle some cayenne pepper on this. That should get his attention. Chinese hot chili oil, Tabasco Sauce, and other similar spicy substances work well also. Finally, if none of these things work, simply yank the leash out of your pup's mouth sharply and command "off" (see p.152) Repeating this procedure only a few times should cure your pup of this habit.

whose approach is consistent with what you've learned so far.

All that having been said, let's get started with your pup's training.

First Things First

There are three items that I view as fundamental building blocks without which your pup's training would get off to a shaky start. First, he must learn to tolerate not only wearing a leash and collar but being directed with it as well. Second, since you'll be using lots of treats in the initial stages of training, your pup must learn to take treats while leaving your fingers intact. Third, your pup should learn an "off" command which will teach him to take his mouth and attention off of whatever he's doing immediately (see p.152 for more information on this command). This you'll need in relation to many of the exercises outlined above. Let's examine these three prerequisites in turn.

Leash training

Most young pups like wearing a leash about as much as I like wearing a tie. While the limitation of a leash on a pup's life is nothing compared to the suffocating limitation I used to experience wearing a tie, from his perspective it's still considerable. Nonetheless, this is a piece of equipment that he must learn to tolerate as soon as possible as it will remain a permanent feature of his experience for the rest of his days. A leash is not only an instrument of control, it is a line of communication, not unlike the cable that brings television into your home, and thus teaching your pup to wear it opens one of your first channels of communication with him.

Of course, your pup doesn't know any of this so you have to teach it to him. Begin by letting him simply drag the leash (a very light weight six footer is the best) around for a day or two so he can get used to the sensation of something exerting slight pressure on his neck. Most pups habituate to this relatively quickly which allows you to take the next step. Pick up the leash and start walking around alongside your pup, still letting him set the course. Occasionally get his attention with a treat and walk backwards, encouraging him to come to you. As he happily bounds in your direction give him a few *very gentle* nudges on the leash and when he gets to you give him his treat. Then allow him to go about his business. This conditions him to accepting those little leash nudges in a very positive context. Continue to do this for a while, exerting increasing amounts of pressure on the leash, but never enough to really make him balk.

Walk with your pup alongside

Back away; put a little pressure on the leash while offering a treat.

Of course, at some point the moment of truth is going to come. He's going to want to go one way and you're going to want to go another. When this happens you'll find your pup bucking and straining like a wild horse or a hooked fish and your most likely response will be to try to drag him to you. While you might be able to pull this off, I wouldn't recommend it. It'll never teach him to walk nicely with you. The trick is to pull and release, pull and release, until your pup starts moving in your direction. In other words, when your pup is struggling against the leash, pull him slightly towards you *for just a moment* and then release the pressure on the leash. The moment you release the pressure coax the pup to you in

As the pup moves toward the treat, release pressure and reward

any way you can — by clapping your hands, showing him a treat and using a high pitched and fun voice, squeaking a toy, whatever it takes — and the moment he takes even a half a step in your direction praise him wildly. As soon as he starts moving towards you back away from him as this will encourage a following response on his part. If, at some point, he balks again, simply repeat the procedure. *Remember, pull, release, and encourage. Do not drag.*

Once the pup starts following you continue to praise and encourage him in every way possible. Use a happy voice to tell him what a good little guy he is, slap your thigh to help keep him focused and occasionally, when he's pretty well at your side, slip him a treat. In fact, slip him a treat whenever he is not too far in front and not too far behind, but nicely near your side. This will teach him that good things happen in this area and encourage him to spend more time there. This, in turn, lays a foundation for heeling later.

Lure with a treat, praise and encourage...

And he'll soon get the idea!

When things are rolling along nicely begin changing directions on your pup. If he wants to go one way, you go another. If he begins to balk again, simply repeat the procedure outlined above. Changing directions begins to habituate your pup to paying attention to you and, of course, attention is the foundation of meaningful communication between you and your pup. Soon you'll find that your pup will learn to understand the meaning of your leash nudges and when you change direction he will work to stay with you.

Learning to take a Treat Gently

Since you'll be using lots of treats in the initial training process it's essential for your pup to learn how to take them from you without turning your fingers into hamburger meat with those little piranha like teeth of his.

Offer your pup a treat...

If his teeth hurt you...

Turn the back of your fingers to him and give him a little bop on the nose...

When he takes it more gently, release the treat.

WHAT KIND OF TREATS?

The best kinds of treats to use in training are soft, chewy ones. Hard, crunchy biscuits take time to eat and the crumbs that fall on the ground tend to distract your pup from training. Soft, chewy treats are quickly inhaled and allow the training process to continue unimpeded.

My favorite treat of all is, believe it or not, string cheese. That's right, the stuff you can buy at the grocery store. It's plain old mozzarella, free of the chemicals, preservatives and other junk you generally find in dog treats. It's easy to tear off tiny little pieces for your pup and it's cheap! If you feel that dogs shouldn't eat people food please read the section entitled Food for Thought (see p.100).

If your pup has digestive troubles or is on a special diet for some reason then, of course, don't use cheese. In this case it's okay to use his kibble for treats. Just deduct the amount you're going to use in training from his meals, throw it in a baggie, and use as needed.

To teach him to take a treat gently hold it tightly between your thumb, forefinger and middle finger (see photos, previous page). Present it to the pup in such a way that he can smell it and lick it but can't get it out of your hand. The point is to try to frustrate him a little in order to see if he will bite at your hand in an attempt to get it. The moment you feel any pain, quickly turn your hand in such a way that the backs of your forefinger and middle finger are up against the pup's mouth and give him a quick, little bop in the nose while saying "ouch" in a mildly reprimanding tone. *You don't have to do this very hard, just enough to startle the pup.* Most often, your pup will take a couple of shocked steps backward, trying to figure out what just happened. Continue to offer him the treat as you just were and now you're likely to find that he'll be much more careful in his next approach. Hold the treat for a few seconds and if you sense that your pup is trying to be very cautious and he's not hurting you, release the treat. In this manner he gets immediate positive reinforcement for taking it nicely and having that happen just on the heels of the reprimand will make it pretty easy for him to understand what you're trying to teach him. Once he's understood this concept try it with him when he's really worked up and teach him that he simply always has to be careful when taking treats, no excuses.

This exercise is in keeping with the zero tolerance biting policy I've mentioned repeatedly throughout this book. It will help teach him self-control even in situations of high stimulation as well as help assure that he'll never hurt anyone accidentally.

The "Off" Command

The "off" (see photos opposite page) command is fundamental to teaching your pup behavior boundaries from his earliest days. Throughout the preceding pages I've referred to following the puppy around with a squirt bottle and com-

When your pup makes a run for the treat...

Command "off" and give a little shove.

When he makes another run for it...

Repeat the procedure.

When he resigns himself and hangs back, reward with a treat and a good "off."

manding "off" just before squirting him for some undesirable behavior. In the next few paragraphs I'll describe how you can teach your pup that "off" means "take your mouth and your body off of whatever you're doing...*now.*"

Begin by sitting on the floor with your puppy in front of you and a pile of treats between you and him. Of course, the moment your pup sees this pile he's going to go for them, thinking that this is a smorgasbord that you've laid out for his immediate consumption. As you see him make a move on the treats quickly take your hand and shove your puppy backwards while commanding "off" in order to prevent him from getting the treats. Undaunted, most pups will come right back for another stab at it. When he does you repeat the procedure, shoving him off firmly without hurting him. After several attempts your pup will most likely pause to consider his predicament by sitting or laying down longingly staring at the treats. The moment you see him pause like this, grab a treat and give it to him while simultaneously informing him what a good boy he's been.

If, after a few moments, your pup takes another crack at it, simply repeat this procedure. Once he's resigned himself to this set of circumstances, make it a little more difficult for him. Start throwing and sliding the treats around in front of him making them as tempting as possible, and whenever he makes another move on them, simply shove him off with the "off" command. It shouldn't take him very long to catch on.

The most important thing during this exercise is to *never, ever, under any circumstances, no matter what* (am I being emphatic enough?) let your pup get even one treat. If he's successful even once in getting a treat from the pile you've commanded "off" on he's no longer going to believe that it's an "off" command that he's learning but that it's a foot race to see who can get to the treat first. This, of course, opens the door to all sorts of problems. He should learn that "off" definitively and always means "you better get away from that, or else."

The "Off" Command – Take Two

Once your pup has internalized all of this, which shouldn't take very long, you can move to the next step in the "off" command. Take a squirt bottle filled with water, a pile of treats and take a seat in front of your pup. Present your pup with a treat and tell him "take it." When he approaches, give him the treat. Then repeat the procedure at least five or six more times until your pup is cheerfully taking the treat from your fingers in conjunction with hearing the "take it" command. Once he's in this flow it's time for a surprise. On the seventh or eight round instead of saying "take it" command "off." At this point the pup is likely to ignore the "off" command and simply go for the treat. At that moment quickly squirt him in the nose and mouth (or diagonally across his nose if he's the sensitive type) with the squirt bottle (which you've been sneakily hiding behind your back). This should startle the pup and he'll most likely back off momentarily. When he does immediately offer him the treat again and say "take it." For the next several iterations, until the pup's confidence returns, allow him to take the treat once again. Then suddenly repeat the procedure. Keep going like this until your pup, upon hearing the "off" command, quickly backs off the treat in order to avoid getting squirted. What you're teaching the pup here is to play "identify the variable." In other words, your pup has to figure out the difference between all those times he simply gets to take the treat and those times he doesn't. Of course, the variable is the command "off." Once again, you'll be amazed at how fast your pup picks this up. If, in the context of all this, you find that your pup becomes resistant to being squirted with water change the contents of your squirt bottle to Bitter Apple™ spray. That should get his attention.

In this exercise there are a couple of key things which you must keep in mind. First, *be sure to hide the bottle behind your back or along your side in such a way that your pup can't see it coming.* You don't want him to learn that your commands are only meaningful when you're armed with this bottle. You want him to think that you have this thing on you all the time to the degree that he might even believe it's simply a part of your body. If he learns that the squirt bottle is the variable he'll start looking for it and won't take you seriously without it. Second, *be sure that there's a slight interval between the time you command "off" and the time you squirt your pup.* After all, the point is to teach him to avoid the correction by backing off in time. If he's getting squirted at the same moment you command "off" he never has a chance to comply and thus avoid the squirt and this, of course, is inherently unfair.

These two exercises will go a long way to helping your pup understand the command "off." By practicing them with him from the earliest times it will be easy for him to generalize this concept into a variety of other situations, such as the ones described in foregoing

COMMON MISTAKES IN FOOD LURE TRAINING

Working with treats makes teaching your pup new concepts incredibly easy. However, there are a few common mistakes you should try to avoid if you want things to go as smoothly as possible.

First, don't move the treat away from your pup's nose too fast. Keep it close to him and just out of reach until your pup is in the position you want. Then deliver the treat.

Second, avoid chanting the command. It's not a mantra. Say it only once just as the pup commits to the behavior. This teaches him to build an association between his body action, your command and a treat.

Third, resist the temptation to force your pup into position. Be patient and give him time to figure out what you want. If you begin pushing him around it will only distract him from what you're trying to teach him.

Finally, be sure to deliver the treat at the exact moment your pup gets it right. Even a few moments later will build the wrong association for your pup and make it difficult for him to learn what you want. Remember, he'll assume that he's being rewarded for whatever he's doing at the moment he gets his treat.

pages. This, in turn, will make teaching him behavior boundaries around your house infinitely easier and thus reduce the level of stress for both of you.

These three exercises, learning to walk on a leash, taking the treat gently and obeying the "off" command, are fundamental to working with your puppy and beginning to integrate him into your life. While leash walking and the "off" command can be taught in conjunction, for the exercises that follow learning to take the treat gently is a prerequisite to everything else. That having been said, let's proceed with some rudimentary obedience exercises.

Hold the treat on your pup's nose...

Sit – Down – Stand

The next set of exercises, sit, down, and stand, forms the basis of all future obedience and takes the form of a drill. While there are three commands, as you'll see in a moment, there are, in fact, six exercises. That is, your puppy is going to learn to go from any one of these positions to any other in rapid fire succession.

And pull it back over his head.

Sit

Let's start with the most basic command any puppy will learn, the "sit." Take a small treat between your thumb and forefinger and present it to your pup. Be sure to keep it very close to his nose so that it keeps his attention. Think of it like a magnet. The further away it is the less effect it has. Once you've got your pup's attention move the treat slightly up and back over his head toward the middle of his back. If you've gotten his attention his head will begin to crane backwards in an effort to follow the treat. If he jumps up for the treat simply say ah-ah in a *mildly*

When his rear hits the ground say "sit" and deliver the treat.

Put the treat on your pup's nose and...

Lure him straight to the ground.

Then pull the treat slightly away to let your pup straighten out.

reprimanding tone, pull the treat away and start over. If he continues to crane his head backwards the laws of physics will quickly convince him to sit in order to maintain a good view of the treat.

As your pup begins to commit to behavior say the word "sit" *once*. It's important that you only say the command *as your pup begins to commit to the behavior*. Do not start chanting the command while you're just holding the treat in front of him. The point here, as with the exercises that follow, is to teach your pup to associate a particular word with a body action on his part and precision timing helps him to put it all together. Again, only say the word "sit" as your pup is committing to the behavior and the moment his little rear end hits the ground give him the treat.

If your pup is one of those that wants to keep backing up as you're bringing the treat over his head try backing him into a corner or gently cupping your free hand over his rear in such a way that it will encourage him to tuck it in (never push his rear end down. This only causes resistance on his part and isn't great for his hips). Run through this exercise a few times until your pup understands what you're asking of him. You'll be amazed at how fast most of them pick it up.

Down

Once you can easily lure your pup into a sit it's time to add the "down" command. With your pup in a sitting position, take another treat and once again place it right on his nose. Once you've got his attention slowly move the treat *in a straight line* from his nose to the ground being sure to keep his attention all the way along. If you find that you've got his nose half way to the ground and he loses interest simply place the treat back on his nose and start over. Once you've got the treat on the ground and the pup's nose is glued to it begin moving it along the ground slightly away from the pup. Generally what will happen at this point is that as he moves to follow the treat he will stretch his little legs out and move towards the down position. As he commits to the behavior in this manner, say the word down and when his elbows hit the ground give him a treat.

From a down position...

Once he's in the down position take another treat and bring your pup back into a sit by luring the treat back over his head, this time at a slight upward angle. Once again, when he commits to the behavior say the command "sit" and deliver the treat when he's fully in the sit position. Once he's in the sit, repeat the down exercise. Go back and forth with these two until you've got your pup doing push ups. Now you've got the first third of your drill in place.

Lure your pup back to a sit.

Now, while the above drill is relatively straightforward, some pups seem to have a hard time getting the down in the way I've just described. Therefore I'll give you a few little tricks in the event that yours falls into this category. If your pup has a tendency to stand up every time you begin pulling the treat to the ground, try *gently* holding his rear end in place as you attempt to lure him into the down position. For many pups, this very little bit of restraint will do the trick.

If your pup tries to stand when you lure him into a down, simply hold his rear end in place with your free hand.

If you find your pup suddenly very concerned about and distracted by your hand on his rear you might try yet another trick. Sit with your legs straight out in front of you and raise one knee up such that you can reach your treat laden hand underneath it. The point is to lure your pup under your knee, which he'll only be able to accomplish by going down. Once he's down try to lure him halfway back up into a sit and then immediately back into a down. This will help teach him the basic concept while he's still more down than up. Once he's done this a few times he'll get the idea and you should be able to simply lure him into a down using the first method described above.

An important thing to keep in mind is that even if you're having a hard time getting your pup to learn the down, *please resist the temptation to force him down by pushing down on his back, hips or shoulders.* This will only cause your pup to fight you as you've engaged his opposition reflex and make progress even slower.

If he always stands from a sit, try luring him down under your leg.

When he's down, reward and...

Return him to a sit.

From a sit, lure your pup...

Into a stand. Say "stand" the moment his hips are level with his shoulders and deliver the treat.

Then return him to a sit, saying "sit" as his bottom hits the ground.

Stand

With your pup in a sit, present him with the treat and *slowly* pull it in a straight line, *parallel to the ground,* away from his nose. *Be sure to keep the treat right on his nose,* perhaps only a millimeter away, so he always thinks he's just about to get it. If you move it too fast your pup will simply sit back and look at you with a puzzled expression. Remember, use it like a magnet. As he keeps reaching for it he'll finally take a step and move into a stand position. As he does say "stand" and deliver the treat.

Once he's in a stand, move him back into a sit and then back to a stand until your pup demonstrates a solid grasp of the concept. Once this is accomplished, add the down command. Have the pup stand, then sit, then down, then sit and then stand again. Now you're starting to put the pieces of the drill together. But there's more.

Down from Stand

To complete the circuit your pup needs to learn to drop into a down out of a standing position. This is an important precursor to an advanced obedience command, the down out of motion, which your pup will learn when he's somewhat older. With your pup in a standing position, present the treat and once you've got his attention slowly move it at a forty five degree angle backward, down and underneath him into the area between his feet. Most pups will respond by reclining down and backwards as if going into a play bow. If all is going well you'll soon find him with his elbows on the ground and his little rear end suspended in the air as if he were still standing. Don't release the treat yet. Just wait. Usually within a few seconds your pup will drop his rear end at which point you say "down" and deliver the treat. If you're having trouble with this please refer to the description of the down above where I lure the puppy under my leg using a treat. Now you're almost there and there's just one more thing to do to complete the drill.

Begin with your pup in a standing position; then lure him to the ground with the treat going into the area between his feet. When his rear finally hits the ground, say "down," and reward with the treat.

Stand from Down

With your pup in the down, present the treat and pull it slightly away from him as you did with the stand from the sit. The only thing you have to do differently is to move the treat away from your pup at a very slight upward angle. This will naturally move him from the down into a stand. A common mistake is moving the treat away from your pup's nose too fast. You'll know there's a problem if your treat is two feet from your pup's nose and he's still laying down. Keep the treat "low and slow." That is, as the treat moves slowly away from the pup keep it relatively low to the ground. If your angle is too steep your pup will either sit or simply look at you in a very confused way. Also, as with all the other excersises in this section, please don't chant. Remember to say the command only at the moment your pup is in the position you wish to reinforce. Then say the word only once and reward. Only after some time, when your pup has demonstrated a solid understanding of the various commands, can you begin to use them as a cue to initiate the behavior. But more on that later.

With your pup in a down, slowly lure him into a stand, being sure to keep that treat right on his nose at all times. When his hips are fully square, reward with a treat.

Putting it all Together

Now you've got all the elements in place to run your pup through the drill. Move him from a stand to a sit, from a sit to a down, from a down to a stand, from a stand back to a down, from the down to a sit, and finally, from the sit to a stand. What you might notice is that while there are three commands, there are actually six exercises. Your pup should be able to move seamlessly from any of these positions to any other. Each of the exercises has real life applications so don't do what so many owners do and focus on just the sit and the down. Your pup has an extraordinary capacity to absorb new material so take advantage of it.

When you initially run your pup through this drill you should reward him with a treat for each performance. However, as he catches on you should start making him do more and more for less and less. Use the same treat to run him through an increasing number of increments of this drill until you can get ten performances for one treat. Use the treat to reinforce the weakest links in the drill. For example, if you're running him through these exercises and you find that the down from a standing position is the weakest element, use your treat to reinforce this piece and thus make it stronger.  Making your pup perform more and more exercises for less and less treats is the first step to weaning him off treats altogether.

WHAT IS A RANDOM SCHEDULE OF REINFORCEMENT?

A random schedule of reinforcement simply means that sometimes your pup gets a treat and sometimes he doesn't. Interestingly, a random schedule of reinforcement is more powerful at reinforcing a behavior, once it's established, than a continual schedule of reinforcement. This has been well-documented and is part of a general learning theory called operant conditioning devised in the early part of the twentieth century by one B.F. Skinner (remember Psych 101?). Consider the following example. If I put you in front of a machine that gave you two quarters every time you put in one you might sit there awhile and double your money. However, at some time you'd get so horribly bored that you'd say to yourself "that's enough" and pack it in. However, if I put you in front of a machine that sometimes gives you a quarter back, more often than not gives you nothing, and at other times gives you thirty quarters back, you might sit there all day long – hypnotized. This, of course, is the whole premise upon which the multi-billion dollar casino industry is built. This is a random schedule of reinforcement. Varying the timing and size of the rewards creates a compelling motivation to perform a behavior. And this psychological principle works as well with puppies as it does with people. If you're interested in finding out more about operant conditioning and learning theory in general please see Karen Pryor's fascinating and easy to read book Don't Shoot the Dog, *and Pamela J. Reid's* Excel-erated Learning, *both available from Direct Book Services at 800-776-2665, Monday through Friday, 7:30 a.m. - 4:00 p.m., PT, or at www.dogwise.com.*

Round and round the puppy goes; where he stops nobody knows!

Adding Handsignals

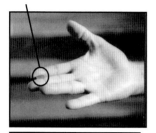

The treat

The proper way to hold a treat when introducing handsignals.

Once you've done several hundred repetitions of these exercises (that won't be hard – doing twenty, five times a day gives you a hundred right there) you'll be ready to add handsignals. This is easier than you think. Dogs are very attuned to body language, both ours and each other's, and learning handsignals is infinitely easier for them than learning verbal commands. Of course, at the end of the day they should be able to do either with equal ease.

In transitioning to handsignals what you'll find is that the treat, which you've been using to lure your pup into position, will follow the same path of travel using the handsignal that it has up to this point already. You'll see what I mean in a moment.

As your pup approaches focus him on the treat with your palm facing him.

Let's start with the "sit" command. Take the treat and place it between your forefinger and middle finger in such a way that you can hold your hand out flat. Hold your hand at your side, fingers pointing toward the floor. Get your pup's attention by saying his name and when he looks at you move the hand with the treat, palm facing up, in a slow sweeping motion past the pup's nose. Make sure he smells the treat as you move your hand past his nose and over his head. While you're doing this say "sit." At this point your pup will have heard "sit" in conjunction with a treat at least a thousand times and will, in all likelihood, plop his little rear end right on the ground. Of course, when he does you say "good sit" and deliver the treat. Henceforth use this movement along with a verbal command and stop luring him the way you've been up to this point. Work on this with both the sit from a standing position and the sit from a down position.

Then sweep your hand upward and as your pup follows your hand he will automatically sit.

The handsignal for the "down" command is exactly the reverse of the handsignal for the "sit" command. With the treat between your fingers as described above, have your arm at your side, elbow bent to ninety degrees. Get your pup's attention by saying his name and move your hand downwards, palm facing the ground. Move the treat slowly past his nose to the ground and command "down." As soon as your pup hits the deck drop the treat between his feet *and make him pick it up off the ground.* You want to begin to condition the pup to orienting to the ground rather than to your hand for the down command. I'll speak in a minute about how to get your pup to go down without needing to bend over. Once again, the handsignal for the "down" should be easy for your pup to pick up if you've laid the foundation with the food lure exercises described above. Practice this with him both out of the "sit" and the "stand" position.

Sweep your hand past your pup's nose...

With your palm facing down, treat between your fingers...

As you go through your repetitions, add speed to this command until your pup anticipates what's coming and starts heading down before the treat even reaches his nose.

And straight to the ground. Release the treat and make your pup pick it up off the ground.

Get his attention with the treat.

Then lure him into a stand and

Reward when done!

The handsignal for the "stand" command is a flat palm facing your pup and moving away from him. The height of the handsignal can be adjusted to your pup's size as he grows. With the treat between your fingers get his attention, place your hand in front of his nose, and slowly move it away from him, *being sure to keep it parallel to the ground.* Command "stand" as you're doing this and pop him the treat the moment he's standing. Again, if you've done your homework to date you shouldn't have a problem with this. Be sure to practice stand both from the "sit" and the "down" positions.

Once you've taught your pup the handsignals try to fade out the food lure exercises as fast as possible. You've set a new standard and you should stick to it. Run your pup through the same drill you have been up to this point, that is, sit, down and stand in rapid succession, but only use your handsignals (with the treat between your fingers, of course) from now on.

Coming back to the "down" command, you'll have to take an extra step to teach him to go down without you having to bend over. Once your pup is easily going down in response to the handsignal try the following routine. Move your hand downward as you have been, but this time, instead of holding your hand down between his feet, continue the sweeping movement with your hand until you can hide it behind your calf (see photos, opposite page). If your pup goes down, quickly toss the treat between his feet, working hard to keep his attention on the treat rather than on your hand. Do this until your pup gets the routine.

Once he understands this exercise and is anticipating the arrival of the treat between his feet rather than out of your hand bend over a little less each time you ask your pup for a down. Of course, whenever he complies immediately toss the treat between his feet. Soon you'll be able to stand up straight, issue the command "down" in conjunction with the handsignal and the pup will go right down. Henceforth this should be your new standard of behavior and you should try not to go back to luring him down.

During the course of this exercise you may come to a point where your pup begins to go down but suddenly stops, as if he's not sure what he's being asked to do. *Resist the temptation at this point to push him down*, chant the command or in

Get his attention and...

Sweep down, hiding the treat behind your leg.

WHAT IS LATENT LEARNING?

Have you ever had the experience of studying some topic only to find after several hours that your brain seems to be, well, full? No matter how much coffee you drink and how much more time you spend cramming, it just doesn't seem to be absorbing. If so, you might also have found that if you just take a break from the whole thing for awhile and come back to it later, it seems to be much fresher and more available than it's ever been. That's called latent learning.

What's happening is that the part of your brain responsible for short-term memory is literally full. It needs some time to process everything to long-term memory and free that space up. Then you're ready for more.

The same thing happens with puppies and good trainers know this. In training there is definitely a point of diminishing returns which is why it's always better to have more short training sessions (as short as two or three minutes although longer is definitely okay) rather than fewer long ones. Hour long classes and private sessions are more for people than their puppies. In short, if you see your pup performing an exercise pretty well, or you feel like you've hit a block, resist the temptation to "do just one more to see what happens." Bring your pup to the best performance of which he's capable at the moment and then take a break. While clinical studies suggest that three hours is the optimal break time, I have found that even a few minutes of down time allow the pup to absorb everything and move forward. Some trainers, wanting to maximize the impact of latent learning, will go so far as to crate a dog an hour before and an hour after training. In this manner the training period is a high point between two rather dull periods and the second crating period facilitates the process of latent learning. See if you can adapt this principle to your situation and enhance your pup's ability to pick up training routines.

any other way help him. *If he looks to you as if he's trying to figure out what you want simply hold your position and remain silent.* I've noticed over years of doing this that pups sometimes just get stuck and freeze, trying to figure out what you want. If you simply give him a little time *without distracting him in any way through sound or motion* he'll often suddenly just go down. Be patient, this can take up to thirty seconds, sometimes even longer. Of course, when he does go down, you release the treat and wildly praise him, highlighting for him the moment he got it right. Allowing him to go through this will help his brain form all the right connections in a way that forcing him never could. However, if you find that your pup is simply distracted and not trying to figure out what you're asking him to do, re-orient him to the treat and start over.

Breaking It Up

When you started out teaching the "sit", "down," and "stand" exercises to your pup it was in the context of a little routine or drill. However, as soon as he shows a relatively solid understanding of the drill you should begin asking him for its various components here and there. In other words, suddenly, for no apparent reason, walk up to your pup with a treat, lure him while asking him for a sit, and give him the treat the moment he does. End of story. A little further on, when he's just sitting somewhere, produce a treat and lure him into a down. Again, end of story. Continue like this with all six exercises and soon your pup will understand them in any context, not just in the context of the drill with which you started.

The Down-out-of-Motion

The down out of motion is a variation on the down out of a standing position. Have your pup moving forward towards you and suddenly present a treat to him and push it slightly underneath him into the area between his feet just as you did with the down out of a standing position. Most pups will put the brakes on and drop into a down relatively quickly.

When your pup is doing this without a problem begin to use an exaggerated hand motion to lure him into the down. Specifically, bring your arm, treat between your fingers, straight up over your head in such a way that your pup can see it and then sweep it down in front of his nose, ending up with it in the area between his feet.

The whole point of all this is to lay the foundation for teaching your pup to drop into a down out of motion and at a distance when he gets older. This is an extremely important safety command that should definitely not be overlooked in your pup's education. The handsignal he will ultimately respond to for this command will be an arm raised straight up in the air (he can see this at a distance) and this exercise conditions him to anticipate going down whenever he sees your arm go up.

Fading Treats out of the Handsignal Hand

While I'm having you use lots of treats to begin training your pup, the ultimate goal is to have your adult dog respond to commands without treats. Thus it's important at some point to begin fading treats away from obedience exercises.

Once your pup has shown a very solid understanding of the sit, down, and stand and is responding to your handsignals with treats, proceed with the following routine. Take one treat and put it between your fingers as you have been. Then take about ten treats in your other hand and hide them behind your back. Give the handsignal just as you have been but rather than reward your pup with a treat from the handsignal hand, reward him with one from the hand behind your back. After a certain number of repetitions reduce the size of the treat in your handsignal hand and continue doing so until there's actually no treat at all in your handsignal hand. During the course of this transition your pup will begin to stop looking for the treat in your handsignal hand, expecting it behind your back and voila, he's now responding to handsignals.

Of course, as time goes by you want to run him through his sit, down and stand exercises using only handsignals and demanding more and more performances for less and less treats.

TEACH YOUR PUP TO LEARN TO EARN

Teaching your pup that he should look to you for direction in all things forms the underpinning of a solid and mutually rewarding relationship. Such a relationship is easily and non-confrontationally cultivated by putting your pup on a learn-to-earn program the moment he begins showing a solid understanding of his obedience routines. What that means is that for every nice thing you do for him, make him do something nice for you first. It could be anything – a simple "sit" will do. The point is that he gives you something before he gets something, a point which will not be lost on your pup.

In other words, if your pup has shown a solid understanding of some element of his training program it's time to hold him to it. For instance, if he's done a thousand sits for you with a treat and you've begun to wean treats away and he suddenly fails to comply you should gently but quickly place him into a sit position using the "sit" component of handling exercise #4 (p.82). Doing so begins to teach him the new concept of "you must" and asking him for such performances in exchange for things that are meaningful to him makes these exercises relevant to his life.

An excellent example of this is found in the following routine. Once your pup has learned the "off" (p.152), "sit" (p.157) and "stay" (p.173) exercises start to incorporate them into his feeding time. Begin by filling his bowl, showing it to him and commanding "off." Then tell him to "sit" and "stay" while you place his bowl down at some distance away. Only release him after he's held his stay for some time and repeat this routine at every meal. Varying the lengths of time you require your pup to stay will teach him to continue to pay attention to you and not anticipate when he will be released. The number of situations in which you can implement such routines are limited only by your imagination and willingness to work with your pup (you've already seen how you can do so in relation to games on p.115) and doing so will very easily and naturally establish you as leader in your pup's mind.

Adding the Stay Command

Once your pup has learned sit, down and stand he should be taught to hold a stay in each of these positions. The down-stay, sit-stay, and stand-stay are described next.

Down-Stay

Once your pup begins to understand the basic idea of the food lure exercises you can add the concept of "don't move from that position until I tell you," otherwise known as the "stay" command.

Let's begin with the "down-stay," a position in which your pup is the least "action-ready," and thus most likely to succeed. Kneel on the ground, take your puppy and place him in a down position using the handling exercise described at the outset of this book (p.77). Be sure to have a pile of small treats next to you but out of the pup's sight. With the pup on the ground and one hand on him to be sure he stays take the other hand, hold it in front of him, palm facing him, and say the command "stay" once. If your pup doesn't move for even a second or two, reach around your side, grab a treat, and give it to him while saying "good stay." Once your pup has taken the treat, again place your hand in front of his face with the handsignal and say "stay" once more.

If at any point your pup begins to struggle and attempt to get up, firmly press him to the ground while issuing a mild reprimand such as "ah-ah-ah." The moment he relaxes release your pres-

First, hold your pup down and give the "stay" handsignal. Then reach around your side, grab a treat (my treats are in the grass and hard to see) and deliver it to your pup.

Stand up, keeping your handsignal out, and move slightly away..

Quickly hand your pup the treat, low and fast to prevent him getting up and...

Move slightly further away and repeat the procedure.

sure and continue as described above. If he holds the position for another second or two, reach around again, give him another treat, telling him "good stay," and then tell him "stay" again. Continue like this but make the period of time between treats longer and longer. Most pups will figure out pretty quickly that if they move, suddenly you're all over them, reprimanding them (mildly) and quickly placing them back in their position. On the other hand, they'll also notice that if they don't move, for some reason you keep giving them treats. "Hmmm," your pup thinks to himself, "just hang out here and they bring me treats or move and have them all over me. What's a dog to do?" It won't take him long to conclude that just staying put is the best decision.

When you see your pup begin to relax into this exercise it's time to increase the level of difficulty. Start not only taking your hand off your pup while he's on a "stay" command, but see if you can actually stand up. Be sure to keep the treats out of your pup's sight otherwise they'll tempt him to break his embryonic "stay." Once you've stood up, quickly reach your pup a treat and tell him "good stay" once more. It's very important, now that you're standing, to *deliver the treat very quickly and at a low angle.* If you don't it's very easy to tempt your pup into breaking his "stay" just when you're about to reward him, as he'll try to meet the treat half-way by getting up.

Once you're able to stand up without your pup breaking his "stay" see if you can take a step back. As soon as you do, if your pup has maintained his stay, return and give him a treat. Remember, if you find your pup getting up to meet the treat halfway you need to bring it in lower and faster. Once you've delivered the treat back off a little further, wait a little longer, return with the treat and so on. Gradually you'll find that your pup will settle into a reasonably decent "down-stay." If, at any point, your pup blows it and breaks his stay you have to issue a firm verbal reprimand *at the absolute moment that he begins to break* (or even if he's just thinking of breaking). Then, without missing a beat, rush in and, as fast as you can, return your pup *exactly to the place* where you had him on a stay. Even if he's only scooted three inches you must return him to the place where you originally placed him on a stay. You cannot permit inching or your pup will never learn that "stay" means absolutely do not move. Once your pup has been returned start over.

You should only release your pup once you've had at least some increment of success and when you do release him it should be with a specific release command such as "take a break." Do not leave your pup to guess when the exercise is over. He should learn that he has to maintain his stay until you release him or give him another command.

During the course of teaching the "stay" command *please never call your pup to come to you. Always release him by returning to him.* If you call your pup to come to you out of a beginning stay command he'll never solidly learn to hold a stay since he'll always figure that you're going to call him at any moment. In other words, he'll be action-ready rather than relaxed in his stay. Additionally, if you call your pup out of a "stay" command with a "come" and then reward him, what have you rewarded him for? Coming, of course. But you're trying to work on the stay command. Let's try not to confuse junior. Only at a much later time, when the now older pup really understands the "stay" command could you occasionally call him to come to you. But definitely *not* during the course of the training covered in this book. As with everything else, you'll be amazed at how fast your pup will pick this up.

The "down-stay" establishes the concept of "don't move from this spot until I tell you" in the young pup and lays the foundation for both the "sit-stay" and the "stand-stay."

The Sit-Stay

The fundamental principles in teaching the "sit-stay" are essentially the same as for the "down-stay," but the level of difficulty is slightly higher because your pup is more action-ready. Nonetheless, he'll get it pretty quickly since you've already taught him the idea of "stay" in a previous context.

Start with your pup *on a leash* and in a "sit" position (see photos on this page). Stand in front of him with the leash handle in your left hand and the leash running between the thumb and forefinger of the right hand. Tucked into the

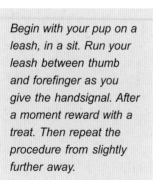

palm of your left hand you should also have a few treats. Use the right hand, with the leash running through it, to show your puppy the handsignal for "stay" and also issue the "stay" command. Stand there for just a moment and then approach the pup to deliver the treat. Again, please deliver it

Begin with your pup on a leash, in a sit. Run your leash between thumb and forefinger as you give the handsignal. After a moment reward with a treat. Then repeat the procedure from slightly further away.

quickly in order to avoid tempting your pup to break his stay and meet the treat halfway. Once you've given him his treat, *ask him to stay again* and back away, this time increasing the distance between you and your pup. Wait a few moments, return to treat him, and then back away again. As you go back and return be sure to increase both the increments of time and the space between you and your pup. You can also move around to different positions in relation to your pup in order to increase the level of difficulty.

If you see that your pup is about to break his stay, immediately cinch up on the leash – *do not yank* – tell him "no" or "ah-ah-ah" and quickly move to reposition him *exactly*

where you started. Also keep in mind, inching is not permitted. Once you've replaced your pup begin the exercise again. As he shows increasing understanding of the concept you may add more time, space, and movement between you and your pup and other distractions as well. Two down, and one to go.

If your pup blows it by breaking his stay, quickly grab him while issuing a verbal reprimand such as "ah-ah-ah," and as fast as you can reposition him exactly where he started and then begin again.

Since this is the most difficult of the stay commands many people ask me what's the point of it in the first place. Here are a few reasons:

- *For wiping his dirty feet.*
- *For bathing him.*
- *For drying him off.*
- *For checking for injuries.*
- *For taking a shot at the vet.*
- *To avoid having him sit or lie down in inconvenient places like wet sidewalks.*

The list goes on but these are a few of the most common applications. Interestingly, I have found that the stand-stay is the most common of the stay commands that I use with my own dog. She is, after all, a Standard Poodle and as such has enormous grooming and cleaning requirement. Her mastery of this command has made it extremely easy to keep her well groomed and lookin' good. By the way, I don't give her one of those fancy poodle cuts but nonetheless she demands a high level of grooming.

The Stand-Stay

"Stand-stay" is the single most difficult stay command because it is the most action-ready. All your pup has to do to break it is to move one foot. However, since he's learned "stay" in two separate contexts now, he should be ready for this.

To teach this command you want to kneel on the floor with your pup in front of you and a pile of treats next to you where he won't see them. Put him in a "stand" by placing one hand under his chin and one under his belly (see photos, opposite page). If you've been doing the handling exercises described previously (see p.82) you should have no trouble with this. Hold your pup in this position until he begins to settle into it. Once he's a little settled take the hand that you've placed under his chin and use it to show him the handsignal for "stay." Wait a moment and if he doesn't struggle or squirm to get away give him a treat. Once you've given him the treat, remind him that he's still on a stay and continue. Pull your hand away again and see if you can begin to move the stabilizing hand out from under his belly. If he begins to sit, use a *mild* verbal reprimand and quickly hoist him back up to the stand. If your timing is good you should catch him just as he begins to sit and slip your hand underneath him before his little butt ever hits the floor. Once he's back in the stay, go ahead and remind him that he is still on a stay.

As with the other stay exercises, your pup should begin to catch on relatively quickly. As he does, once again, add time, distance and distractions. One additional thing you should condition your pup to is to tolerate a body exam while he maintains a stand-stay. He probably won't be ready for this until he's four and a half or five months old, but you should be working with an eye towards this goal.

When working with stay commands be sure to hit all of them equally with special emphasis on areas where he's weak. Throughout your pup's life you'll find a variety of situations that will demand one or the other of these commands and if you haven't practiced them all you may find yourself wanting.

Hold your pup in a stand...

Remove both hands, give signal and...

and show him the hand signal.

Stand up and begin moving away.

When steady, reward with a treat.

If at any point your pup breaks his stay, quickly return him to the stand-stay position, hold him there and start over.

Circling your Pup While He's in a Stay

One of the things you should be working towards in your "stay" training is to be able to walk in a circle around your pup. This is the most difficult of the early exercises since your pup will be tempted to turn around to keep an eye on you. Since "stay" means "don't move until I tell you something different," this is a big no-no.

In order to teach him to maintain his stay while you circle him place your pup in his best stay position, approach him and hold a treat squarely in front of his nose. Keep it there without releasing it while you circle him and when you've gone all the way around and are back in front of him, release the treat. Repeat this procedure several times until your pup seems to have the hang of it. Once you're okay with this try holding the treat a little further away from your pup's nose

Continue to hold the treat on his nose as you make your way around and deliver when complete. Repeat this several times

With your treat on his nose, start to circle your pup.

When you've finished the first few circles, try holding his attention with the treat in the handsignal hand. With this wider circle complete, deliver the treat and re-issue the "stay" handsignal.

while circling him and again release when you're in front of him. When this is solid, try simply holding the handsignal for stay in front of his face while you circle him and deliver the treat with the opposite hand when you've completed your circumambulation. Once you're able to do this consistently without your pup breaking his stay you can start increasing the radius of the circles around your pup as well as the number of circles you do before he gets his treat. Once he's able to perform this exercise in one of the "stay" positions, add the other two as well. Soon you'll be on your way to having a really solid "stay" command.

All that having been said, let's now take a look at the total opposite of stay, which is the come command.

Keep your pup focused on the treat in the handsignal hand and make the circle again.

and going, delivering the treat only after you've completed the circle. Then repeat in ever widening circles.

Keep going...

The Come Command

The one obedience item that generates the most frustrated phone calls from hapless owners concerns their dog's recall or "come" command. To develop a bullet proof recall takes a great deal of work and persistence but the payoff is that your adult dog will be able to experience the pleasures of off-leash living without having

RECALL NO-NOS

Below I have listed the major infractions with which people unwittingly destroy their pup's ability to learn a solid recall.

Never call your pup to come to you and then reprimand him. If you need to reprimand him for something he did "over there" go over there and do it. Otherwise your pup will think, "he called me, I came and got yelled at. I'm not doing that again."

Never call your pup to come to you if you have to do something to him that he views as unpleasant. If you have to put him in his crate, give him a bath, pull some mats out of his coat, or have the vet give him a shot, once again, go and get him.

During the early stages, only call the pup to you when you are prepared to reward him. In other words, only call him in a training situation with the word "come." No frivolous recalls please. If you'd like to encourage him to come to you you can always say "let's go" and clap your hands. But please reserve the word "come" for times when you are really working with him and prepared to set him up to succeed and reward him for it.

Please do not chant the command at him endlessly. Set your training situations up so that your pup hears the command once and then something happens. To a puppy, "come-come-come" sounds a lot different than just "come."

Do not assume that just because your very young pup comes when you call that he necessarily understands the command. Most puppies will come to you when you make any interesting sound and they may even have an inkling of the "come" command. However, they are also quite dependent on you at this point. If you do not systematically teach and reinforce the recall as outlined in this section, when your pup grows older and less dependent on you his "come" command will evaporate like the San Francisco fog in a midday sun.

Avoiding these common mistakes and pro-actively pursuing the exercises outlined in this section will set the stage for your pup to develop a bullet-proof recall.

to surrender the pleasures of living by getting hit by a car.

To teach your pup a solid recall you must first teach him precisely what the word "come" means. I continue to be amazed at the number of people who assure me that their dog understands the "come" command when, with a little investigation, it becomes clear that the dog, at best, has a vague idea. You must systematically teach your pup specifically what "come" means before you can expect or demand compliance.

THE IMPORTANCE OF TONE OF VOICE

The proper and effective use of your voice is extremely important when attempting to communicate with your pup. Consider for a moment that from your pup's standpoint there is a stream of sound coming out of your mouth all day long, most of which has no relevance to him. In order for him to understand that some of those chunks of sound are actually intended for him you have to help him out.

First, when you want to get your pup's attention, look at him. Second, preface your communications with his name. Then, find a special tone of voice that is sufficiently different from your ordinary speech for your pup to be able to pick up that difference. The tone should be somewhat assertive yet upbeat and positive. Then, when you've got his attention follow through with an instruction, don't just stand there. Too many owners run around after their pups mindlessly chanting their names in relation to absolutely everything. The only thing the pup learns is to tune them out altogether.

With respect to tones of voice, there are three which your pup will readily identify. A high-pitched tone of voice is interpreted as an invitation to play. An ordinary tone of voice is considered instructional and a low-pitched tone of voice is considered a reprimand. While this makes intuitive sense some folks get in trouble here. For instance, when a woman gets upset, her voice tends to go up which can result in a pup interpreting a reprimand as an invitation to play. The same is true with kids. If you fall into one of these two groups you'll have to make an extra effort to deepen your voice if you intend to reprimand your pup. On the other hand, men can tend to use a gruff, low-pitched tone of voice, even when giving ordinary commands, often making a pup feel the need to offer excessive displays of submission. Guys can also tend to have difficulty praising their pups in a high-pitched, playful way. Lighten up, fellas.

The long and the short of it is to be very conscious of how you communicate with your pup. Remember, high-pitched equals fun, ordinary is instructional, and low-pitched is reprimanding. Keeping these simple rules in mind will do wonders to facilitate meaningful communication between you and your pup.

Start with your pup as young as possible and teach him to associate the word "come" with something wonderful, such as a treat (or a toy, or praise if he's not food motivated). Do this randomly and as follows. At some point, while your pup is exploring his environment, take a treat and present it to him. As he begins to focus on it back away from him, encouraging him to follow you. As he begins to move in your direction, *in an enthusiastic tone* of voice say "come." As with the other exercises, please initially only say the word "come" *once the pup has committed to the behavior.* Keep in mind that at this point "come" is not a command, merely a training exercise, and that you're simply trying to build an association for him.

Once your pup has moved in your direction a few

To start teaching the come command 1) walk up behind your pup and 2) get his attention with the treat and say "come." Then 3) back away from him luring him towards you with the treat and 4) raise your treat hand to lure him into a sit and 5) finish by grabbing his collar and delivering the treat.

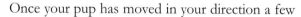

steps, guide him into a sit using the treat as a lure, grab his collar with one hand, give him the treat with the other and then immediately release him to go back to what he was doing.

There are a few elements that bear dwelling on here so let's examine each in turn. First, always guide your pup into a sit. If you start out like this pretty soon he'll offer it immediately. This, of course, is the point. When you call your pup you'd like him to stop what he's doing and come sit in front of you eagerly awaiting your next instruction.

Second, grab his collar. A great many dogs hate having their collar grabbed because to them it signifies your control and thus the end of the fun. Grabbing your pup's collar each time before you release the treat teaches him to completely ignore this movement on your part and thus any potential future games of keep-away are stopped before they start.

Third, immediately release your pup after you've given him his treat. Most people only call their dogs to come to them when it's time to leave the park, when they're further away from them than they're comfortable with, or when they're into something they shouldn't be. Thus the pup learns that come means "the end." The end of what? Of whatever fun he was having! Is that what you want him to learn? Of course not! You want him to learn that "come" is one of the best things that could ever happen to him. How do you do that? By giving him his treat and *immediately* releasing him to go back to whatever it is that he was doing. This way it's a net gain for your pup: he gets both the treat and a return to whatever activity he was having fun with.

Practice this exercise repeatedly throughout your day and it won't be long before you won't have to stick the treat on his nose to come over to you. As soon as he hears the command he'll come charging. Once your pup is covering some distance to come to you be sure to *begin praising him the moment he even thinks about coming.* I can't overemphasize the importance of this. Too many owners wait for their pup to arrive in front of them before they get any praise. But by that time all the action is over! Praising him the moment he even thinks about coming helps him to focus on you, and continuing to praise him – *wildly* – until he gets to you literally builds a verbal bridge between where he is and where you are. You see, from your pup's perspective there are a million distractions between the two of you. If you keep him focused on you with vigorous and ongoing praise he'll ignore all that other stuff and appear in front of you in short order. Otherwise it's very easy to lose him.

Now that your pup recognizes and responds to the come you can add a few games that will strengthen this concept for him. The first game involves getting two or more family members to simply call the pup back and forth between them. If you're doing this exercise with just two people it won't be long before your pup begins to anticipate the next recall and automatically heads for that person without being called. When this happens you should not reward your pup but rather have the person whom the pup just left call him again. In this manner he will learn that he should come to whoever called him rather than simply running back and forth between the two of you. Of course, if there are three or more people involved this is a non-issue. Simply call the pup back and forth randomly.

A second game you can play is hide-and-seek. Set up the same back and forth recall game just described but as the pup is running towards one person for his treat, the other should move to a different, slightly difficult to locate spot, and then call the pup back. When your pup gets to the spot

PLAY 'N TRAIN

Teach your pup that training is fun by interspersing training with play. Fool around with him a bit then run through a few sits and downs, using the same upbeat attitude that you did during your play. Then go back to playing and a short while later run him through something else. Mixing it up like this makes it difficult for your pup to tell the difference between playing and training and thus, of course, radically lowers his resistance to working with you. Not only that, but it will drive all of his play energy directly into his obedience exercises, bringing out a much higher level of performance than if you did only straight training sessions.

from which you originally called him and doesn't see you there he will go looking for you. It's okay to call him a second time if you feel he's trying but is having a hard time finding you. Of course, when he does find you, you should immediately throw a party. Give your pup the treat, praise him wildly, both verbally and physically, and then release him. When the other person calls him back they, of course, will have done the same thing, that is, hide in a different place. This game adds a new dimension to the exercise for your pup and will make it even more exciting for him. It's also a great example of how you can combine play with obedience to make the whole experience more fun for all involved.

Courtesy: Erica Mannion

Recalls in the Puppy Play Group

Once your pup has learned this in and around the home you should begin practicing it in different contexts as well. For instance, if you've got him in a puppy playgroup for socialization you have a wonderful training opportunity. Basically, the exercise is the same as described above. While your pup is playing, simply take a treat, present it to him squarely on his nose and, as he focuses his attention on it, back away a few steps while saying "come." *Once again, be sure to praise your pup wildly as he begins to move towards you.* In such a distracting context this is doubly important. By now your pup should be sufficiently familiar with the concept that he'll know what to do. Again, when he gets to you, guide him into a sit, grab his collar, give him the treat and immediately release him back to what he was doing.

In the context of a puppy playgroup you may have to make a couple of minor adjustments to the recall routine due to the intense level of distraction. First, bring killer treats. Whatever you've been using as treats at home, ramp it up. If you've been using cheese, move up the food chain to hot dogs or even cooked chicken. Having your pup hungry for the playgroup (in other words, don't feed him beforehand) wouldn't hurt either.

Remember, you want him to associate coming to you with extraordinarily pleasurable consequences. Second, if, despite your killer treats, you're having trouble getting your pup's attention, begin by reaching in, grabbing his collar and orienting him toward the treat with a slight pull on the collar. Keep in mind, *this is designed only to orient the pup toward the treat, not to drag him toward you.*

TREATS AND THE FINICKY PUP

If your pup is relatively un-motivated by treats you'll have to take some steps to help motivate him. This is a relatively simple matter. First, do not feed him before his training session, especially if you're going into a class context. If you're going into a training situation that's heavily distracting you can even skip two meals. Hungry dogs always work better, even if you're not using treats in training. Second, bring truly killer treats that he absolutely never sees any other time. I don't care if you have to use medium rare steak. Whatever it takes. The combination of these two elements should motivate your pup. Of course, the idea is not to starve him. Once your training session is over you can make up the difference in the food he didn't get earlier. You just want to make sure that he's really hungry at key moments to facilitate learning.

Once your pup begins to catch on make the exercise more challenging. Try calling him to you without putting the treat on his nose from a very short distance, say three feet. Again, *the moment he **begins** to come, praise wildly,* deliver the treat and release him. As your pup's aptitude for this grows, slowly increase the distance. If you're in the playgroup with a partner you can add another wrinkle, *as your pup shows an increasing capacity to perform this exercise.* Have one partner stand on one side of the room holding the puppy. Then have the other partner show him killer treats and walk into the middle of the room, the pup's attention still riveted on the treats. Once in place some distance away from the pup the partner with the treats calls him and the partner holding him lets him go. The idea is that the pup will run past all the other freewheeling little furballs straight to partner #2 in order to get his treat. Then, of course, he's free to play with his pals. Once this is well in hand, the partners can stand on opposite ends of the room and try the same exercise. The puppy will then have to run the gauntlet of the entire room in order to get his reward. Doing so will build his focus and determination to get to you – valuable components of a solid recall.

You might wonder what you should do if half way to you your pup decides to take a detour. Immediately issue a verbal reprimand such as "no" or "ah-ah-ah," run in and grab your pup by the collar as described above, re-orient him to the treat and lure him to the position from which you initially called him. If you find that he's too distracted to finish the exercise you should evaluate whether you've gone too far too fast, whether the treats are good enough, and whether your puppy is hungry enough.

Once again, please keep in mind that these are training exercises, not full on commands at this point and that you should move ahead in increments with which your pup can be successful. Trying to jump ahead too fast will only set you back. Remember, catch him doing something right rather than setting him up for failure.

Practicing Recalls with your Puppy Outside

As I mentioned above, you should practice your recall exercises with your pup in as many contexts as possible. This would include the great outdoors. Once your puppy is past his inoculations he'll be undertaking a great many more excursions in all sorts of contexts outside. Outdoors, of course, is the single most important place you're going to need to have your pup come to you. So be sure to practice all the exercises outlined above with your pup under open skies. This shouldn't be too difficult since by the time you begin taking him outside he should have had plenty of exposure to the recall concept. Actually, the only thing you're going to do differently outside is use a leash.

Flexi Leashes come in a variety of sizes and styles.

In this context a *twenty-six* foot retractable Flexi-Leash is my preferred piece of equipment. The idea, of course, is that your pup has most of the mobility of an off-leash dog without the actual opportunity to run away. Practice your recalls as described above, adding distance and distractions as your pup is able to handle them. If, at any point, your pup ignores your recall you may use *gentle* leash nudges to get his attention and orient him towards you. Keep your basic rules in mind: use killer treats, bring a hungry pup, start praising wildly the moment he even

Establishing A Cruising Radius

By limiting your pup's off-leash freedom until he has firmly grasped the "come" concept you not only prevent him from figuring out that he can blow you off, you also help him establish what I call a cruising radius. In other words if, during his early life, he gets habituated to being able to go no further away from you than twenty six feet, the length of a retractable leash, he'll tend to view that as, shall we say, his orbit with you. That's not to say that when the time comes and he does get to go off leash he won't go further away than that. He probably will. However, he will always seek to re-orient himself back to his comfort zone with you, and usually sooner rather than later. In other words, it's highly unlikely that he'll ever be one of those dogs that takes off three hundred yards down the beach and doesn't show his face again until thirty minutes later.

thinks about coming, and release him the moment you've delivered the treat and grabbed his collar.

This, of course, brings up a very important question: when should you take your pup off the leash outside? My benchmark is generally when he will respond to you ninety-five to ninety-eight percent of the time, *without a nudge or correction on the leash*, no matter the level of distraction. Only then should you begin to even think about giving him off-leash freedom. I am definitely not a big fan of giving puppies off-leash freedom too soon in their lives. Often the consequences are that he never learns a solid recall during his formative period, learning rather all the strategies to avoid coming when called. As the pup matures with this knowledge it can become quite difficult to train him to come *reliably* later in life, short of using extreme measures such as remote training collars (electronic collars).

In other words, knowing that without a leash you are helpless (this is called line-wise) is information that your dog can definitely live without, but once he's learned it, it's extremely difficult for him to forget. Given the fact that your pup will be with you for many years, I feel that depriving him of outdoor, off-leash freedom for as long as it takes for him to learn a solid recall, is a small price to pay for the years of off-leash freedom he will ultimately have. Remember, it's your responsibility to safeguard him in situations where he cannot grasp the consequences of his actions for himself. The fact is that if you stay the course your pup will never learn that he could actually run away from you because he will rarely, if ever, have had the opportunity to do so. How long will it take before your pup gets to this point? Every dog is different, so there's no telling. But again, I have no problem depriving the pup of outdoor off-leash freedom even until he's eight or nine months old, if it means that for the rest of his life he will be reliable.

The only exception to the above rule would be if you have available a completely fenced in and thus safe outdoor area for your pup to play in. In that case the same rules outlined for the puppy playgroup would apply.

This, of course, brings up the question of what to do if you feel that your pup is ready for a little off-leash freedom based on his previous performance and he suddenly decides to blow you off. If you've called your pup to come and he ignores you, you must respond immediately. Once it's clear what's happened promptly issue a loud and firm reprimand. Sometimes clapping your hands and running away from your pup can change everything in your favor. If your pup suddenly has a change of heart and moves in your direction you must praise vigorously. When he returns, treat as usual and release your pup. Then try him again within thirty seconds to see if he learned anything. If he ignores you a second time, put him back on the leash. He's clearly not ready for this kind of freedom.

If your pup, rather than coming to you after hearing the reprimand, either takes off running or simply ignores you, your situation is somewhat more precarious. On the one hand, *you absolutely must not chase your pup.* This only teaches him that he's faster than you, more information he can definitely live without. On the other hand, you can't just let him get away with it either. This would send entirely the wrong message. Therefore, you must find a middle ground. As with the above, issue a firm and loud reprimand and move toward your puppy *deliberately and without running.* While

HIDE AND SEEK

I've already talked about playing hide and seek with your pup in the house (p.186) but this is a game that can be used to your advantage outside as well. If you're at the phase in training where you're experimenting with a little off leash freedom for your pup it's good policy to occasionally, when he's not paying attention, ditch behind a tree or hill and hide from him. When he turns around to check in on you, guess what, you're gone! This can come as quite a shock to some pups. Keep an eye on him as he goes looking for you and if it's clear that he hasn't a clue as to your whereabouts go ahead and call him again to orient to him to you. When he finds you, throw a party! Give him treats, profusely praise him and then continue on your walk. Repeat this little drill several times per walk and your pup is going to learn to pay much closer attention to what you're up to.

Photo: Carol Irvine, Irvine Photo

Lola is resting in the grass after a fun recall session.

doing so, continue to issue your reprimand: "no…no…no…no" as you steadily pursue him, *deliberately and without running.* Your pursuit should be Terminator like – steady and resolute. Continuing to issue the reprimand while you're tracking him down will allow you to reprimand him after the fact, since your unbroken verbal barrage builds a bridge back to the original infraction. In other words, he'll understand that all the trouble started when he ignored you. Now, you might find that your pup will dash about for awhile, seeking to avoid you, but if you persist you will eventually corner him. When you do, give him a solid scruff shake and firmly tell him "no" several times before putting him back on the leash. This will teach him that once he's blown you off, there's no going back. You will always ultimately get him, without giving him the satisfaction of a chase game, and his off leash fun will be over. Conversely, if he'd just come to you he would have gotten his treat and he'd already be back to what he was doing. Yes! Your pup is smart enough to figure that out.

Once you've got him back on the leash drill him some more and then try him again. If he then pulls a stunt like this again, he's clearly not ready for off-leash work. Go back to working him on the Flexi-Leash for some time longer.

Finally, if you find that your pup is becoming increasingly reliable on his outdoor off-leash recalls, make it a policy to call him at regular intervals. Too many people take their pups to off-leash play areas and for forty-five minutes or more don't interact with them at all. What the pups tend to learn is that in that context the owner is irrelevant. You never want your pup to learn that you are irrelevant in any context, including his most fun play area. Simply calling him periodically, rewarding him, and releasing him, serves to remind him of your importance and relevance in his life.

How fast your pup learns a reliable recall depends entirely on the particulars of your puppy as well as the consistency of your training. However, with most pups teaching a solid recall will take you several months past the end of the critical socializing period. Despite the fact that this is technically beyond the scope of this book I wanted to address it at least partially because of its extreme importance.

The Stop Command

This command is another extremely important one for your pup to learn because of the safety features it helps to build into him. Unlike the recall, however, this one is quite easy to teach.

As you're walking with your pup on leash and on your side or slightly ahead of you, simply command "stop," give a slight nudge on his leash, and the moment the somewhat startled pup stops tell him "good stop," and give him a treat. After a moment say "let's go," and keep moving. Repeat this numerous times and at random intervals and soon your pup will stop the moment he hears the word. Of course, whenever he does he gets a treat.

Once he understands this concept, try getting him to stop when he's behind you. You can quickly stop most pups in their tracks by holding a "stay" handsignal out in front of their face and taking a sudden step or two in their direction. Again, once the pup stops, praise and treat, wait a few moments and then release him.

Once he's understood this from both positions begin asking him for it from any position relative to him that you might like. You'll be amazed at how fast your pup learns this command. In the context of the stop

ONCE IN A LIFETIME

The "stop" command is one of those things that if you use it successfully once in your dog's life, it was worth teaching. Years ago I had a gorgeous German Shepherd named Smokey who I'd done a great deal of training with. Part of it included the "stop" command. One day I was standing with Smokey in my front yard and at a moment when I wasn't paying attention (yes, dog trainers blow it too occasionally) he darted across the street after a cat. Luckily he made it across the street okay but now he was full tilt in pursuit of his feline prey. Of course I didn't want to call him to come to me – that would mean having to cross the street again – and I didn't want him to continue to go after the cat. So at the top of my lungs I yelled "STOP" and to my surprise (this was the real deal, after all) he froze and looked at me. Then I commanded "sit-stay" and walked over and got him. Of course I praised him profusely for his prompt compliance and breathed a very big sigh of relief. It was the only time I ever had to use the "stop" command in a real life situation, and man, was I glad I had it.

command it doesn't particularly matter whether your pup stands, sits, or lies down. It only matters that he stops. Once he's absorbed this you can add the sit, down, or stay command as you wish.

Preliminary Heeling

Heeling is the very last command I introduce with young puppies, because frankly, it's the least important. Walking on the leash nicely is very important and was covered at the very outset of this section (p.148). However, formal heeling is a precision exercise that requires enormous concentration on the parts of both pup and owner. Therefore I don't generally introduce it until near the end of the critical socializing period and until I've had a chance to cover everything else discussed so far.

You should introduce heeling in precisely the same way that you've introduced everything else: with a food lure. My favorite food lure for this exercise is string cheese for reasons that will become obvious momentarily. Take a piece of string cheese several inches long and place it in your palm so that your thumb is holding it in place in such a way that your pup can lick, nibble and pull pieces off of it without taking the thing out of your hand. Then simply present the treat to your pup and lure him around in the heel position by your *left* side (close to you with his shoulder blades aligned approximately along your pant seam) while chanting "heel, good heel, heel, good heel…" Chanting the command at this introductory stage is permissible since heel is a command that has duration over time. However, like all other props, it will be faded out in due course. If you're doing this correctly, your pup will be tearing off small pieces of cheese while he's in the heel position during which time he'll be building the association with the command, which you're chanting. As he gets habituated to focusing

WHY HEEL ON THE LEFT?

Clients always ask me this question and the truth is it doesn't really matter on what side you heel your dog. However, heeling on the left is a universally accepted convention so if you plan to participate in any formal dog activities I suggest staying with this convention.

"How did this start in the first place?" you might ask. Well, most of dog training has its origins in the hunting traditions of days gone by. Since most people are right handed they carry their gun on the right making it much more convenient to have their dog on the left lest they should accidentally blow his head off. Well, how's that for another useless canine factoid?

on your hand you don't have to keep putting it on his nose. Hold your hand a few inches above his head and have him look up at it for a few moments as he follows you around. Then reach down and give him a treat, pull your hand up for a little while longer and after a few moments reward again. Stay with this routine until you can keep your pup focused on your hand for thirty or more seconds.

If your pup falls out of the heel position use very small, gentle leash nudges accompanied by the word "no" to bring him back into position and refocus him on the treat. Do not say the word "heel" while issuing nudges on the leash. Remember, you want him to associate the word heel with heeling, not with being corrected. Along with leash nudges try patting your leg or tempting him with the treat in order to lure him back into position. Once he's back in the heel position he will once again find the cheese in your hand and hear you saying that special word.

Hold a piece of string cheese like this. Then follow the photos below.

Start with the treat directly on your pup's nose, then...

Lead with the treat periodically to get him used to distance from the it while maintaining focus on it.

Finish with a sit by pulling your treat over your pup's head.

Changes of Pace

Once he's okay with this begin adding changes of pace to be sure that your pup is really working to stay with you and doesn't just happen to be walking alongside (there is a big difference). While heeling, suddenly slow down to a very slow walk. If you've got him focused on the treat he should have no trouble slowing down with you. If he's not as attentive as he could be and ends up ahead of you use a *very mild* leash nudge with a gentle "no" or "ah-ah-ah" to alert him to the fact that he's off the mark. Once he's slowed down to your pace, resume rewarding with the cheese.

When you've walked slowly for a little while suddenly pick up the pace and start walking very quickly. Keep him focused on the treat and he should stay with you. Nudge on the leash and pat your leg if you have to until you can bring him back into position and then resume with the treats once more. With each change of pace you should say the word "heel" with special emphasis. Soon your pup will be working hard to stay with you.

Directional Changes

At this point it's time to introduce changes in direction. Both right and left about turns (180°) require not only sudden changes of direction from your pup, but changes of pace as well. Thus they can be a little difficult to teach.

 Let's start with right turns. The trick on the right turn about is to get your pup to speed up as you move into the turn. You see, while you're only more or less pivoting in place your pup has to move all the way around you on the outside. In order to encourage him to do this make sure that just as you begin to move into the right turn you have the treat squarely on your pup's nose. You want to lure him through the turn with it and let him have a big bite *as soon as the turn is completed.* If your pup learns to anticipate a large chunk of the treat the moment the right turn is done he will begin to drive into the turn in anticipation thus giving him the speed required to keep up with you and to avoid lagging.

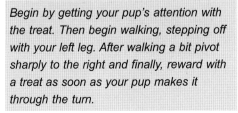

Begin by getting your pup's attention with the treat. Then begin walking, stepping off with your left leg. After walking a bit pivot sharply to the right and finally, reward with a treat as soon as your pup makes it through the turn.

On the left turn the problem is exactly the opposite. You have to cover the space around your pup and since you should not have to speed up, your pup must learn to slow down. With your pup nicely along your left side (he can't be too far ahead or you'll have a hard time turning left) pull the treat slightly back and over his head, almost as if you were going to ask him for a "sit." At the same time take an exaggerated step with your right leg, lifting your knee high into the air a couple of times. This gives your pup a visual cue that something is about to change. At this point, move into your turn, keeping your pup focused on the treat and close to you. Once your turn is completed deliver the treat and resume your regular walking.

In both right and left turns it's important to make the turns nice and tight, almost pivot-like. This is important as it dramatically highlights the directional change for your pup. If you take wide, meandering turns, what's expected will be less clear to him.

THE LEFT TURN

Then take an exaggerated step with your right leg while pulling your pup back with the treat hand.

Lead your pup with the treat.

Continue to keep him focused on you as you straighten out again.

Stationary Heeling

In this final heeling exercise you want to teach your pup that when you say heel, no matter where you are, he should immediately come to you and align himself along your left side (or your right, if you've chosen that side).

Have your pup "stay."

In order to effectively work with this exercise your pup's sit-stay should be reasonably solid. Place him in a sit-stay, walk away and turn your back on your pup. Then hold a treat out along your hip and ask your pup to "heel." Try focusing him on the treat and luring him with it. If that doesn't get him moving try a pat on your leg. That usually gets them going. Once your pup is moving in your direction try to orient him to the treat and lure him into a sit position next to you with it. Once he's sitting next to you say "good heel," give him the treat and tell him to "stay" again.

Then command "heel" and lure with the treat.

Once again, walk away, turn your back to him, but this time return to your pup and tell him "good stay." Tell him to "stay" again and repeat the procedure. The reason for this is that at this early stage his "stay," no matter how good, is not bullet-proof. Thus, if he begins to anticipate that every time you tell him to stay and walk away, it'll just be a moment or two before you have him heel, he'll be so action-ready that his stay will become very weak. Therefore, for each "heel" you practice, reinforce three stays.

Once your pup catches on try positioning yourself at various angles in relation to him. This will make him work ever harder to find the heel position next to you. The point of this little exercise is to help solidly define the heel position for your pup as an imaginary box next to your leg. That is, it doesn't matter whether you're just standing there, or walking or turning; "heel" means "alongside, right now!"

Reward when pup sits in heel.

Always Finish in a Sit

Whichever version of heel you're practicing, you should always have your pup finish in a sit. The easiest way to teach this is to issue the command "sit" *about one second before you actually come to a halt* while simultaneously luring the pup into the position with the treat. The reason that you want to ask him to sit one second before you stop is that it will give him time to process your request and end up sitting perfectly aligned with you when you come to a halt. If you stop and then ask him to sit, in the beginning he will invariably take another step and end up sitting slightly ahead of you. This, in turn, can become a bad habit that you'll only have to work later to correct.

You might ask yourself, "who cares if he sits alongside or two feet out ahead of me." Well, consider if you come to some kind of intersection such as a bike path or even a street. If your dog is in a heel and you suddenly stop because you've seen some bicyclists racing along the path, but your pup takes another step or two…well, need I say more. The point is, your pup should learn that when you ask him to heel he should remain glued to your side and pace himself perfectly to your activity.

There is a good deal more to say about heeling but it falls beyond the scope of this book. The exercises outlined above should be easy for your pup to assimilate by the end of his critical socializing period and lay the foundation for more serious heeling in the future.

Fading away Treats

As your pup learns to focus on the treats you've got in your left hand begin holding your hand a little higher up than he can reach for so that he'll just stare at the hand as he walks. If he tries to jump at the treat, quickly pull it away, give your pup a little snap on the lead and tell him "no." Then try to refocus him on the treat in your hand and keep going. Once he's walked with you for a few seconds without jumping up to get the treat quickly bring your hand down and let him take a bite. Then, just as fast, bring your hand up and out of reach again. Ultimately you should be able to hold your hand in a closed fist at about your belt level with your pup focused on it and awaiting the next treat. This is the first step to fading treats out altogether and by the end of his critical socializing period he should be able to walk in a heel for several minutes with only occasional treats.

Photo: Mike Wombacher

Sierra, a four month old Shar-pei.

Teaching your Pup to Accept Handling on the Leash

As you move into adolescence with your pup you can rest assured that he's going to challenge your authority to place demands on him. In other words, you're going to ask him to do something and he's going to look at you as if he'd never heard the command before. What are you going to do then? Pull out a better treat? Definitely not! You're going to demand compliance. Now, as I've already discussed, in the early stages of training you'll be demanding compliance to commands your pup has shown a solid understanding of by using the handling exercises outlined earlier (see p.73) to move him quickly into position.

However, as he gets older you'll be increasingly relying on your leash as a way to give your now adolescent pup information about his behavior. In order that this doesn't come as a surprise to him you want to introduce this concept as he's nearing the end of his critical socializing period. By this time the relationship between the two of you should so firmly rooted in the principles of trust and respect that this shouldn't be a big problem. You should learn to use your leash to place your pup in the sit, down and stand commands. Let's take a look at each in turn.

The Sit

In order to demand a sit from your pup using the leash have him stand in front of you and, with the leash clip under his chin, command "sit" and *gently* pull the leash towards you at a forty-five degree angle while applying steady pressure to the pup's neck. At the same time hold a treat in the hand holding the leash. *Please do not yank the leash! This is not a punitive correction!* You will observe that the forty-five degree angle of the leash combined with a little steady pressure will create an opposition reflex in your pup which he will use to move his rear end in the exact opposite direction of the leash pressure, in other words, toward the ground. Once you see that he's pretty well committed to sitting immediately release the pressure on the leash and praise him with a generous dose of physical affection as well as his treat.

The same approach will work to get your pup to sit while he's lying down. Again, simply pull the leash away from him at a forty-five degree angle using steady pressure and the opposition reflex will cause him to pull backwards and up. Presto, chango…he's sitting again. Praise, treat and you're done. Once he catches on he'll learn to interpret such leash pressure as a command and soon you'll be able to eliminate treats and resort only to physical praise.

Begin by pulling your pup's leash toward you with slow, steady pressure. **No yanking!** *Hold a treat in front of his nose and when he finally sits, deliver the treat and release the pressure.*

The Down

If your pup is in a sitting position take the leash and gently pull it with pressure going from his neck, again at an approximate forty-five degree angle away from him and towards the ground while commanding "down." Again, simultaneously lure with a treat and *please do not yank the leash! This again is not a punitive correction!* He may resist for a few moments but most pups will give in in relatively short order and fold like a card table. Doing this exercise on a somewhat slick floor, such as hardwood, linoleum, or smooth concrete, is helpful for the pup as he can easily slide into the required position.

First, pull your treat and leash down and away from your pup(treat is in leash hand). Then begin exerting slight downward pressure on the leash while still luring with the treat. Finally, when your pup is down, release the leash pressure and reward.

From the standing posture the exercise is quite similar. Again, exert downward pressure on the leash leading with a treat, this time into the area between your pup's feet at about a forty-five degree angle while saying "down." This time you can help him out by placing your free hand just in front of his shoulder blades and exerting a little pressure at the same forty-five degree angle. This should give you plenty of leverage to move your pup into the down and, of course, once he's there praise him.

Holding the treat and leash together, pull/lure into a down and...

Release pressure and reward as soon as the down is complete.

The Stand

With your pup in the sit position, stand in front of him, run your leash around the outside of your right arm, (with which you'll be giving the handsignal) command "stand" and then move your arm away by giving the stand handsignal. This should exert slow, steady pressure on the leash, which should remain perfectly parallel to the ground, away from your pup. Most likely he will resist by pulling backwards but between the treat in your hand and steady pressure on his leash he'll soon be on his way up. As you continue pulling away from your pup, say the command "stand" until he gives in and stands up. The moment he begins to stand, immediately release pressure on the leash and praise him with a treat and affection. Once again, be very gentle here. *Please do not yank the leash! This is not a punitive correction!*

From the down position this exercise is essentially identical. The only difference is that instead of keeping your leash perfectly parallel to the ground you'll want to pull it away from your pup at a slightly upward angle which is necessary to move him from lying down to standing up.

Puppies, Children and Obedience Exercises

As with the handling exercises described above (p.73), children should learn to work with your pup on obedience exercises once you've taught the pup a solid understanding of them. When your child is working with your pup try to focus the pup on your child. If your child is too young to follow through on a behavior you should be there to help him and teach your pup that your child carries the weight of your authority. For more information on dogs and children please see my book *There's a Baby in the House: Preparing your Dog for the Arrival of Your Child.*

This concludes the obedience section of this book. The exercises outlined above are designed to give you and your pup a solid foundation in basic obedience commands which you both can use as a springboard to move into the more serious training of his adolescent period. If you've followed my directions carefully you should have a pup that's happy to work with you since all of the exercises have been based primarily on positive motivation. In short, training should have been fun rather than adversarial for the both you. With that concluded there are only a few more things to say.

Begin by wrapping the leash around the back of your treat hand. Then pull the handsignal hand away from your pup, exerting pressure on the leash while luring with the treat. When your pup arrives in a solid stand, release the leash pressure and reward.

LOOKING TO THE FUTURE

Introduction

As your pup grows out of his critical socialization period he is rapidly heading toward adolescence with all that that implies. With respect to this I'd like to leave you with a few thoughts.

As you continue to pursue your training I would encourage you to find training situations that utilize and build upon the methods introduced in this book. As your pup matures and his understanding of the training exercises solidifies you should be steadily working towards fading treats out altogether and replacing them with other motivators such as toys and physical praise. By the end of the first year all training props, from treats and toys to collars and leashes, should have been faded away and your dog should be responsive under any situation without the benefit of any tools.

I see good things ahead for us!

That having been said, I'd like to add a couple of admonitions. Often clients will ask me when their dog will be old enough to walk with them off the leash through the city. My unequivocal response always is *"never."* In other words, no matter how well trained your dog is *it's simply never appropriate to walk him off the leash in the city under any circumstances, period.* It only takes one mistake, and yes, even the most well trained dog can make mistakes, for something to go terribly wrong. Every year I get three or four new clients who lost their last dog because he was off the leash in the city. "For ten years I walked him through my neighborhood," one teary client recently shared, "and one day he saw something, I don't even know what, and he ran out in front of a bus." Anything can happen at any time. Please always keep in mind that your dog has no concept of the potential consequences of his actions and he's relying on you to protect him. And that is the purpose of a leash, not to restrict your dog's freedom, but to protect his life. You don't walk a two-year old through the city without holding his hand, and as a general rule, if you wouldn't do something with your two-year old you probably shouldn't do it with your dog either.

Along the same lines, I would urge great caution in leaving your dog tied out in front of stores. For starters, *never do this with your puppy*. Dogs get stolen every year, by the thousands. You never know to what larcenous heart your pup's big innocent eyes might appeal while you're in the store.

Even as your dog gets older I would advise great care in leaving him unattended in public. Once every couple of months I'll get a call from a client who came out of a store only to meet an angry passerby who informs them that their dog tried to bite him, or worse, actually did. Of course, they have no idea what happened so they'll have to take the stranger's word for it. The point, of course, is that while you're in the store you have absolutely no idea what's going on with your dog. There might be kids teasing him. There might be an aggressive dog attacking him. He might be startled by some unexpected event in the street. He might be anxious about your absence and in a fearful state he might do things he otherwise might not. In all these scenarios the one common factor is that you're not there to protect him. If you're going to tie your adult dog out in front of a store be sure to keep an eye on him from inside and not to leave him out there too long. When I occasionally leave my dog tied out it's usually the length of time it takes to get a cup of coffee or for my wife to check out a "sale" sign in a store. And even then I keep half of one eyeball on her at all times. Please don't play games with the life of your dog. Active and careful supervision should be the mainstay of your effort to keep your dog safe.

Spaying and Neutering

Finally, as your pup approaches adolescence the issue of spaying or neutering will certainly arise. I usually advise my clients to take care of this around the age of six months. I have heard all the arguments for waiting until later (they should have one heat or one litter, and the hormones will help them fully realize their growth potential are the most common ones) and frankly find none of them convincing. The fact is that the negative behavioral and societal consequences far outweigh any potential benefit that might be gained by not spaying or neutering early.

Consider for a moment that the nation's animal shelters are overflowing with dogs whose only fault is that there is not a home for them. Most of them are not mean, vicious, or sick, simply unwanted. The number of dogs destroyed annually is in the millions. Every backyard litter contributes another six to twelve pups to this problem. Even if you think that you've got good homes for all the pups your dog might generate, research has shown that by the end of the first year half the pups from backyard litters are in shelters awaiting lethal injection. Sad but true. Even if your pup is so adorable and well temperamented that you want to have his genes passed along please leave breeding to the professionals. They will guarantee the continuity of the line that produced your pup. You needn't worry.

Photo: Carol Irvine, Irvine Photo

Lola is definitely not camera shy.

Aside from all this there is the issue of hormone related behavioral problems, primarily in male dogs. When a male dog becomes adolescent his testosterone level spikes to something on the order of ten times the level of a fully adult male dog. Because of this he starts emitting a scent to all other males in the area that lets them know a young upstart is on the prowl – an invitation for them to put him in his place. He might as well be wearing a sign that says "kick me." He will get bullied and harassed until he either submits or fights back. Alternatively your dog might be filled with an irrepressible urge to challenge every other dog in the neighborhood. Either scenario can lead to long-term behavioral problems with aggression. If your dog ends up being aggressive this will put a serious limitation on his quality of life and, in extreme cases, might cost him his life altogether. Spare yourself and him the headache and neuter him early. After all, if he's not going to get to use the equipment why let him keep it and drive both of you crazy?

THE ROAD TO A PERFECT PUPPY OR THE PUPPY PRIMER TIMELINE

In the preceding pages you've read everything you'd ever need to know in order to produce a puppy that will grow up to be a wonderful companion dog. As a way to conclude this book and pull all these pieces together I'd like to organize them along a continuum in order to help you see where along your pup's learning curve all the pieces fit. Below I have outlined a day by day, week by week, breakdown of what to do with your pup. Its purpose is to give you a sense of the order in which you can introduce and develop everything described so far.

My beginning assumption is that you're starting with a pup that's about seven weeks old, in my view, the perfect time to introduce him into your life. However, even if your pup is significantly older than this the essential roadmap is the same. In other words, whether your pup is seven weeks old or thirteen weeks old, you should introduce everything outlined in this book just the same. You'll simply have to adjust the time frame to the realities of your situation.

Let's see what's on the schedule for today.

In the same vein, every puppy is different with respect to how fast they catch on to the various items presented in this book and, of course, you'll have to work within the confines of your pup's aptitude. Keep in mind what I've said several times throughout this book: work at a pace that your pup can handle. Set him up to succeed. Too much too fast will only hold both of you back.

The long and the short of it is that the timeline laid out below is not to be viewed as being carved in stone and carrying the weight and authority of Biblical tablets. Rather, it is a guideline that you'll have to adjust to the particulars of your own situation. Please keep that in mind as you work your way along this roadmap through the joys and occasional frustrations of puppyhood.

Week 1 (Pup is seven weeks old)

Day 1

- Pup arrives at home.
- Be thoroughly familiar with housebreaking routine and have a developed strategy ready (p.43)
- Be thoroughly familiar with the first section of this book, Before Getting Started, (p.13)
- At night, have crate next to bed and follow nighttime procedure for elimination (p.56).

Day 2

- Begin with handling exercises one through four (p.77).
- Be diligent with your housebreaking effort – remember, confine, supervise and regulate.
- Begin conditioning pup to wearing a leash and collar (p.148).
- Teach your pup how to take treats from your hand gently (p.151).
- Introduce his chew toys and work diligently to prevent inappropriate chewing (p.106).
- Begin introducing alone time and work them into each day from here forward (p.134).
- Remember, your puppy needs his sleep (p.24).

Day 3

- Continue with all of the above.
- Begin letting puppy drag leash around the house (p.49).
- Introduce "off" command (p.152), first exercise only.
- Begin introducing house noises in very small increments, such as the hair dryer (p.138).
- Begin preventing jumping up on you or others (p.92).
- Call puppy pre-school and make appointment for puppy

playgroup (p.130). These classes usually fill up and the more lead time you have the more likely you'll get in a group as soon as two sets of inoculations are in your pup.

- If you're going to use a doggie day care center (p.133) do the same.

Day 4

Courtesy: Erica Mannion

- Continue with all of the above.
- Go to next level of leash training – take leash and begin walking around with it (p.148).
- Slowly begin introducing the bathtub and water (p.137).
- Start taking your pup outside in your arms and introduce him to people (p.123).

Day 5

- Continue with all of the above.
- Introduce the sit/down/stand routine (p.157).
- Introduce tie downs (p.49).
- Introduce "off" command, second exercise (p.155).

Muffin's first full bath!

Days 6 & 7

- Continue with all of the above.

Weekly Recap

A lot has happened this week and you're probably in a state of shock. Who knew it would be this much work? However, by the end of the first week you've also gotten quite a bit going. You should have your housebreaking routine well in hand, your pup is learning to accept a leash, you've introduced some handling exercises, a few people, the bathtub, the "off" command, the sit/down/stand routine and more. You've also begun to teach him not to jump up on you and to handle alone time. And finally, you've made arrangements for a puppy play group. It's been a busy week! Let's see what week two has in store for you.

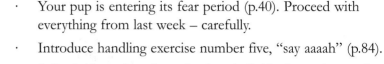

Week 2 (Pup is eight weeks old)

Day 1

Courtesy: Erica Mannion

- Your pup is entering its fear period (p.40). Proceed with everything from last week – carefully.
- Introduce handling exercise number five, "say aaaah" (p.84).
- Split sit/down/stand routine into individual exercises and begin asking your pup for them randomly (p.170).
- Introduce the "come" command (p.182).

Day 2

- Introduce nail clipping (p.140).
- Finish leash training – pup should learn to wear it without a problem (p.148).

Erica and Portia

- Begin using the umbilical cord approach to supervising your pup around the house (p.49).
- This will begin to enable you to teach him about furniture rights (p.105).

Day 3

- Continue with all of the above.
- Actively begin using "off" command enforced with a squirt bottle as you supervise your pup in order to teach him your house rules.
- Don't forget to keep working with him in and around the bathtub.

Days 4 - 7

- Continue with all of the above.
- Begin taking your pup outside in your arms and getting him used to the sights and sounds of your city (p.127).
- If you can crate your pup in the car, begin introducing short car rides (p.141).

- Throughout this week be sure to slightly increase the amounts of time your pup is asked to be alone in his crate.
- Begin reprimanding behaviors such as jumping up (p.92), and nipping at you and your clothing in play (p.95).

Weekly Recap

This week your pup entered its fear period (see p.40) so while you should continue with his education, you should do so carefully and avoid any major traumas. You're adding a handling exercise and slightly broadening his life both indoors and out.

Week 3 (Pup is nine weeks old)

Day 1

- Introduce handling exercise number six, the muzzle grab and forehead kiss (p.86).
- Introduce the "down-stay" command (p.173).

Day 2

- Decide what your house rules are going to be in relation to such things as the dinner table, room restrictions, etc.
- Continue to test the "off" command in various contexts around the house. Remember to keep your squirt bottle handy.
- Move towards introducing handsignals for sit/down/stand by placing treat between fingers (p.166).

Day 3

A teensy-weensy Manray

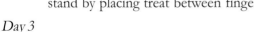

- Begin introducing proper table manners (p.98).
- Continue with car rides, adding time.
- Visit the doggy day care center (if you're going to use one) and your puppy socialization situation and make sure you like them.

- Pay an introductory visit to the groomer (p.141).
- Continue exposing your pup to the sights and sounds of the city.

Days 4–7

- Add more water during bathing routine.
- Begin introducing the hair dryer (p.138).
- Introduce exercises designed to prevent object guarding (p.111).
- Familiarize yourself with the rules for games and begin introducing them (p.115).

Weekly recap

Things are moving right along. You're beginning the process of introducing elements of his life that will be with him for a long as he's with you. Be diligent in adding small increments to your desensitization exercises and remember never to push your pup past what he can tolerate. Be sure to slowly increase the amount of time your pup spends alone.

Week 4 (Pup is ten weeks old)

Day 1

- Continue with everything from the preceding weeks, yet remain cautious as your pup is still in his fear period.
- Introduce handling exercise number seven, rough him up (p.86).
- Start keeping a close eye out for counter surfing (p.101), digging (p.109), excessive barking (p.96), and other problematic behaviors and work to correct them.

Day 2

- Add levels of difficulty to your recall exercise including calling the pup back and forth between you and the hide and seek game (p.190).

· Introduce the "sit-stay" command (p.176).

Day 3

· Introduce heeling (p.194).

Days 4 – 7

· Continue to let your pup meet people in safe environments (p.123).

· Continue to expose your pup to city sounds in a safe manner (p.127).

· Make check list of everything you're working on with your pup and make sure you hit everything every day.

· Increase water in tub, proximity to hair dryer and handling and clipping of toes until you can put him through a full bathing and grooming routine.

· Begin working simple tricks into your training routines (p.120).

Weekly Recap

The most important thing this week is to take stock of how far you've come. Your pup has begun to absorb an enormous amount of information and you know for yourself now that anyone who says you can't teach a dog anything before he's six months of age doesn't know what they're talking about. Because your pup is learning so much it's a good idea to make a checklist to be sure you're hitting everything each day.

Week 5 (Pup is eleven weeks old)

· It's the last week of your fear period.

· Keep working with everything from the preceding weeks – you've got a full plate now.

· Puppy biting should be minimal at this point.

- Pay another visit to the groomer.
- Introduce "stand-stay" (p.178).

Week 6 (Pup is twelve weeks old)

A patriotic puppy!

- The fear period is over – hurrah!
- This would be a good week to enter a puppy socialization program, either a playgroup (p.130), or a day care (p.133).
- Introduce obeying the down command without having to bend over (pp.168-169).
- Lots of emphasis on down out of motion (p.170).
- Begin, as you deem appropriate, the first step of fading treats out of handsignal hand by rewarding only with treats from behind back (p.171). Take your time, no big hurry here.
- Begin working with your pup on recalls in the puppy playgroup (p.187).

Week 7 (Pup is thirteen weeks old)

- Continue with everything you've learned so far. You should have a nice rhythm going with your pup.
- Your pup should be sleeping through the night without needing to eliminate.
- Your pup should be easily able to handle two hours of quiet time in the morning and two in the afternoon.
- Pay another visit to the groomer.
- Add increasing levels of complexity to the recall in the puppy playgroup (p.187).
- Add complexity to your heeling exercises by adding directional changes (p.196), changes of pace (p.196) and stationary heeling (p.199).

Week 8 (Pup is fourteen weeks old)

- All your friends should be duly impressed with the progress your pup is making. The truth is that your little pup will, at this point, have more training in him than most other adult dogs that you'll run into.

- Continue working your pup with everything you've learned so far and begin gently demanding the exercises he's learned so far. For instance, if he really knows sit well and he doesn't do it, make him using the methods you learned in handling exercise number four (p.82).

- Begin to put your pup on a learn-to-earn program (p.172). That is, for every nice thing you do for him ask him for one of his newly learned exercises first.

- Introduce the "stop" command (p.193).

- Begin adding elements that will move you towards eliminating treats in heeling (p.200).

Week 9 (Pup is fifteen weeks old)

- Your pup may, at this point, have all his shots in. Begin going to doggie parks with him while he's on a Flexi-Leash™ and start practicing recalls outside (p.189).

- Begin teaching him to accept more handling on the leash (p.201).

- Begin walking him around the city and introducing him to as many odd situations as possible. Look for any signs of fear and work on desensitizing routines (p.127).

Week 10 (Pup is sixteen weeks old)

- Begin to look for a boarding kennel and make arrangements for a short stay for your pup (p.136).

- Begin looking for a dog walker if you're going to use one.

- Continue diligently working him with everything that he's

learned so far and begin creatively running your obedience drills together so that your pup can move smoothly from anything he's learned so far to any other thing.

Weeks 11 & 12 (Pup is seventeen to eighteen weeks old)

· During these weeks everything is essentially the same as during week ten. Continue working with him and you will be ready for him to move to adolescence.

· Find a trainer whose methods are compatible with what you've learned in this book and continue your pup's education. You're well on your way to a wonderful canine companion.

Recap

By the time you're through implementing everything outlined above you'll be amazed at what your pup has learned. You'll now know first hand that anyone who tells you that you can't teach your pup anything meaningful before he's six months old simply doesn't know what they're talking about. You'll have discovered what an eager learner your pup is and how much fun it is to train together and all this will set the tone for the rest of your lives together.

And there you go! An obedient, attentive, and most importantly, happy puppy.

Conclusion

In the foregoing pages I have described a program that, if followed diligently, will produce a dog that will be well adapted to the demands of canine life in a 21st century human world. Your puppy will be housebroken, learn to respect you and your family and accept most any type of handling he might encounter during the course of his life. He will also learn how to behave properly in relation to other dogs, accept the variety of people and noises he might be exposed to on an average day, handle time alone, visit the groomer, and stay at a boarding kennel all without incident. Additionally, he will have begun to learn the obedience commands necessary for you to control him and thus assure his safety in any situation. In short, he will be a dog that will be easy to integrate into every aspect of your life and thus be a pleasure to live with rather than a burden.

Making the commitment to spend the time required and exert the effort called for in order to successfully execute this program is an investment in the life of your puppy. If you make this investment during his critical socializing period and carry it through for the duration of his first year you'll have to do very little for the rest of his life in order to maintain everything your pup learns during this timeframe. A very large return on your investment indeed! Certainly the years of love and companionship that you'll receive from such a dog are worth a little work on the front end. I wish you and your puppy the best and hope that this book has been helpful

APPENDIX

Plants Toxic to Dogs

A

Alfalfa
Almond (pits of)
Aloe Vera
Alocasia
Amaryllis
Apple (seeds)
Apple Leaf Croton
Apricot (Pits of)
Arrowgrass
Asparagus Fern
Autumn Crocus
Avocado (fruit & pit)
Azalea

B

Baby's Breath
Baneberry
Bayonet
Beargrass
Beech
Belladonna
Bird of Paradise
Bittersweet
Black-eyed Susan
Black Locust
Bleeding Heart
Bloodroot
Bluebonnet
Box
Boxwood
Branching Ivy
Buckeyes
Buddhist Pine
Burning Bush
Buttercup

C

Cactus, Candelabra
Caladium
Calla Lily
Castor Bean
Ceriman
Charming Dieffenbachia
Cherry (pits, seeds, & wilting leaves)
Cherry, most wild varieties
Cherry, ground
Cherry, Laurel
Chinaberry
Chinese Evergreen
Christmas Rose
Chrysanthemum
Cineria
Clematis
Cordatum
Coriaria
Cornflower
Corn Plant
Cornstalk Plant
Croton
Corydalis
Crocus, Autumn
Crown of Thorns
Cuban Laurel
Cutleaf Philodendron
Cycads
Cyclamen

D

Daffodil
Daphne
Datura

Deadly Nightshade
Death Camas
Devil's Ivy
Delphinium
Decentrea
Dieffenbachia
Dracaena Palm
Dragon Tree
Dumb Cane

E

Easter Lilly
Eggplant
Elaine
Elderberry
Elephant Ear
Emerald Feather
English Ivy
Eucalyptus
Euonymus
Evergreen

F

Ferns
Fiddle-leaf Fig
Florida Beauty
Flax
Four O'clock
Foxglove
Fruit Salad Plant

G

Geranium
German Ivy
Giant Dumb Cane
Glacier Ivy
Golden chain

Gold Dieffenbachia
Gold Dust Dracaena
Golden glow
Golden Pathos
Gopher Purge

H

Hahn's Self-Branching Ivy
Heartland Philodendron
Hellebore
Hemlock, Poison
Hemlock, Water
Henbane
Holly
Honeysuckle
Horsebeans
Horsebrush
Horse Chestnuts
Hurricane Plant
Hyacinth
Hydrangea

I

Indian Rubber Plant
Indian Tobacco
Iris
Iris Ivy

J

Jack in the Pulpit
Janet Craig Dracaena
Japanese Show Lily
Java Beans
Jessamine
Jerusalem Cherry
Jimson Weed
Jonquil

Jungle Trumpets

K

Kalanchoe

L

Lacy Tree Philodendron
Lantana
Larkspur
Laurel
Lily
Lily Spider
Lily of the Valley
Locoweed
Lupine

M

Madagascar Dragon Tree
Marble Queen
Marigold
Marijuana
Mescal Bean
Mexican Breadfruit
Miniature Croton
Mistletoe
Mock Orange
Monkshood
Moonseed
Morning Glory
Mother-in-Law's Tongue
Morning Glory
Mountain Laurel
Mushrooms

N

Narcissus

Needlepoint Ivy
Nephytis
Nightshade

O

Oleander
Onion
Oriental Lily

P

Peace Lily
Peach (pits & wilting leaves)
Pencil Cactus
Peony
Periwinkle
Philodendron
Pimpernel
Plumosa Fern
Poinciana
Poinsettia (low toxicity)
Poison Hemlock
Poison Ivy
Poison Oak
Pokeweed
Poppy
Potato
Pothos
Precatory Bean
Primrose
Privet, Common

R

Red Emerald
Red Princess
Red-Margined Dracaena
Philodendron
Rhubarb
Ribbon Plant

Rosemary Pea
Rubber Plant

S

Saddle Leaf Philodendron
Sago Palm
Satin Pothos
Schefflera
Scotch Broom
Silver Pothos
Skunk Cabbage
Snowdrops
Snow on the Mountain
Spotted Dumb Cane
Staggerweed
Star of Bethlehem
String of Pearls
Striped Dracaena
Sweetheart Ivy
Sweetpea
Swiss Cheese Plant

T

Tansy, Mustard
Taro Vine
Tiger Lily
Tobacco
Tomato Plant (green fruit, stem, and leaves)
Tree Philodendron
Tropic Snow Dieffenbachia
Tulip
Tung Tree

U

Umbrella Plant

V

Virginia Creeper

W

Water Hemlock
Weeping Fig
Wild Call
Wisteria

Y

Yews—
e.g. Japanese Yew
English Yew
Western Yew
American Yew

IN CASE OF EMERGENCY

Symptoms of plant poisoning include refusal of food, swollen tongue, pale gums or tongue, abdominal pain, convulsions and diarrhea, severe and persistent (not occasional) vomiting.

If a poisoning should occur try to identify the plant. Call poison control and your veterinarian immediately and bring sample to the vet if possible. **If** *it is necessary to induce vomiting, one to two teaspoons of hydrogen peroxide orally should do it.*

Kansas State University's Poison Control Hotline (For Animals Only) - *Phone: 785 - 523-5679*
This is a free service.

Animal Poison Control Center @ 1-800-548-2423

Toxic Household Products

A variety of household compounds are potentially toxic. The worst offenders include:

Antifreeze - Ethylene Glycol is found in antifreeze and is odorless, colourless, sweet and deadly. Clinical signs include vomiting, depression, abnormal righting reflexes, generalized or focal seizures and coma and commence anywhere between thirty minutes to twelve hours after ingestion.

Chocolate

Onions

Lime

Tylenol and Ibuprofen

Drain cleaners as well as other household cleaning agents.

Kerosene and fuel products (obviously)

Poisons and insecticides

Note: If your dog has ingested caustic poisons *do not induce vomiting!* Attempt diluting the toxin with Milk of Magnesia in water, an egg white in one cup of water, or regular milk.

Pet Emergency First Aid Books & Videos
Books: Puppy Owner's Veterinary Care Book, *James DeBitetto;* Puppies for Dummies *by Sarah Hodgson also has a good section on First Aid.*

For videos I found the following on the web:
Phone/Email: 1-888-380-9966,
order@apogeevideo.com
Cost: First Aid for Dogs ($19.95),
First Aid for Cats ($19.95),
Combo: Dogs and Cats ($34.95)